The Rockwool Foundation Research Unit

The Unemployed in the Danish Newspaper Debate from the 1840s to the 1990s

Bent Jensen

University Press of Southern Denmark
Odense 2008

The Unemployed in the Danish Newspaper Debate from the 1840s to the 1990s

Study Paper No. 21

Published by:

© The Rockwool Foundation Research Unit and University Press of Southern Denmark

Copying from this book is permitted only within institutions that have agreements with CopyDan, and only in accordance with the limitations laid down in the agreement

Address:

The Rockwool Foundation Research Unit

Sejroegade 11

DK-2100 Copenhagen Oe

Telephone   +45 39 17 38 32
Fax   +45 39 20 52 19
E-mail   forskningsenheden@rff.dk
Home page   www.rff.dk

ISBN   978-87-90199-15-9
ISSN   0908-3979
August 2008
Print run: 300
Printed by   Special-Trykkeriet Viborg a-s

Price: 160 DKK, including 25% VAT

Foreword

Since the beginning of the 1990s, the Rockwool Foundation has given high priority to supporting research into labour market conditions. For example, in 1991 the Foundation launched a competition for the development of new and unconventional proposals to combat unemployment, which was at a very high level in Denmark at that time. This interest in the labour market has been maintained ever since, with the result that new research results relating to the Danish labour market have been published every one to two years.

A few years ago, in connection with this long-sustained interest, the Board of the Rockwool Foundation decided to allow the Foundation's Research Unit to carry out a project involving the analysis of the debate in Danish newspapers on the unemployed that has been going on ever since the establishment of a system of representative democracy in the country. During this lengthy period, a historic milestone was passed in April 1907 with the Act of Parliament on recognised unemployment funds. The centenary of this landmark legislation was celebrated last year.

The project was placed in the hands of Bent Jensen, MA, who had previously carried out analyses of material from Danish newspapers published over long periods – for example, his analysis of the newspaper debate on immigration to Denmark, published in 2000 under the title *De fremmede i dansk avisdebat fra 1870'erne til 1990'erne* ("Foreigners in the Danish Newspaper Debate from the 1870s to the 1990s" – also the title of a short English version published in 2001), Spektrum, 2000.

The aim of this new analysis was to cover the most important elements of the political press, and thus to paint a coherent picture of the way in which Danish newspapers had discussed the subject of the unemployed over a period of 150 years.

Prior to the publication of this book, three working papers have been published by the Rockwool Foundation Research Unit during the period 2006-2008. These have presented the detailed documentation on which this more synthesised presentation is based. A summary volume in Danish, entitled *Hvad skrev aviserne om de arbejdsløse? Fra 1840'erne til 1990'erne* (What the Newspapers Wrote about the Unemployed from the 1840s to the 1990s), was published in 2008 by Gyldendal. This summary included a new quantitative analysis of the extent of the debate at various periods The present volume, which is intended for an international readership with an interest in Danish history in general and press history in particular, is based on the Danish summary text.

Throughout the analysis work for all these five publications, the Research Unit has had the help and advice of Jette Drachmann Søllinge, MA, who has read and commented on the manuscripts from her perspective as a press historian. She has also written the material on the history of the press during the period covered. Aage Huulgaard of the Danish National Directorate of Labour has also contributed comments on the basis of his comprehensive knowledge of the legislation and administrative practice in the area, while Niels Ploug, Director of Social Statistics at Statistics Denmark, has drawn on his extensive knowledge of the Danish labour market to add further comments. Dr Ole Hyldtoft, Associate Professor at the University of Copenhagen, has also commented on Bent Jensen's analyses on the basis of his exhaustive knowledge of large parts of the period under consideration and of Danish industrial history. Finally, Lars H Andersen, sociology student, has read the manuscript in order to comment on its accessibility and clarity.

My thanks on behalf of the Research Unit go to all these commentators, and to all our other collaborators who have provided assistance in the course of the preparation of these publications.

The analyses in this book are based on newspaper articles which have been gathered together using the Danish Royal Library Newspaper Reading Room. The assembling of articles has been carried out by a group of student assistants working under the supervision of Bent Jensen. Monika Dinek, Iben Fritze, Jens Nielsen Gram, Pernille Parsberg Hansen, Rigmor Vogt Johnson, Christine Karen Kofoed, Tea Malthesen, Rikke Lea Mertz, and Line Brix Overlund have all worked on the project for varying lengths of time. Everyone involved has put in many hours of work at the Royal Library, and I thank them for their great endurance in their work in front of the screens in the newspaper reading room.

Ilona Csiky and Iben Marianne Overgaard, librarians at Statistics Denmark, have been very helpful in assembling the secondary literature that has been used in the analyses.

At the Research Unit itself I owe special thanks to Mai-britt Sejberg, who proof-read the manuscript and prepared it for printing. Johannes K. Clausen and Peer Skov, students of Economics, assisted with the collection of the texts of various laws and other information, as did Mark Gervasini Nielsen, MSc, who also provided research assistance for the quantitative part of the study in Appendix 1.

Finally, I would like to express my gratitude to the Rockwool Foundation and especially to Tom Kähler, Chairman of the Board and Elin Schmidt, Director, for their continued great interest in the work of the Unit – including the preparation of this volume.

Copenhagen, August 2008   *Torben Tranæs*

Contents

1. Introduction: Objectives, definitions, and an overview of press history 7
1.1. Concepts and definitions 7
1.2. An overview of Danish press history, and the selection of newspapers for the study 8
1.3. Translation of the newspaper titles 11
References 12

2. The Debate from 1848 to 1907 13
2.1. The prelude 13
2.2. The debate in 1848, the European year of revolutions 13
2.3. The 1850s and 1860s: An interlude 16
2.4. A Socialist agenda 18
2.5. The debate in the 1880s and 1890s 22
2.6. A breakthrough 23
References 24

3. The debate from the first law on state-recognised unemployment funds in 1907 until the 1940s 25
3.1. The climate of opinion at the time of the adoption of the law 25
3.2. The debate during the First World War 27
3.3. The debate in the 1920s 32
3.4. The debate during the Great Depression 33
3.5. Occupation and Liberation 37
References 40

4. The period from 1950 to the mid-1990s 41
4.1. The early 1950s 41
4.2. The remainder of the 1950s: The "islands of unemployment" 45
4.3. The long period of prosperity, 1959-73 49
4.4. The oil crisis, autumn 1973 53
4.5. In the grip of the crisis, 1976-82 57
4.6. The debate on unemployment under a centre-right government, 1982-84 60
4.7. After 1993: the debate under a Social Democrat-led government 64
4.8. Conclusion 67
References 67

Appendix 1 69
A quantitative analysis of the debate in *Berlingske Tidende* and *Social-Demokraten/Aktuelt* 1900-1990 69
The data used 69
Results 71
The unemployment figures 73

The relationship between the unemployment figures and coverage
    in *Berlingske Tidende*...75
The relationship between the unemployment figures and coverage
    in *Social-Demokraten/Aktuelt* 77
Summary and conclusions 78
References..79

Appendix 2...81
An overview of the newspapers in the survey 81
References..87

Publications in English from the Rockwool Foundation Research Unit..............89

The Rockwool Foundation Research Unit on the Internet...................................93

1. Introduction: Objectives, definitions, and an overview of press history

The aim of this book is to present an overview of how the most influential Danish newspapers dealt with the theme of "the unemployed" over a period of 150 years. Taken as a whole, the analyses presented here are intended to illustrate how the debate unfolded through the period from the ending of absolute monarchy in the spring of 1848 to the turn of the millennium. In the course of this progression, we shall see how the arguments presented in the various newspapers shifted on the subject. The presentation is based on a research project carried out by the Rockwool Foundation Research Unit over the period 2005-2008.[1]

There was a gradual general change over the whole period of 150 years whereby relatively greater numbers of Danes became waged employees instead of leading lives as independent workers – as peasants and as smallholders – than was the case around 1850. The opportunities Danes had to protect themselves financially against hard times thus diminished. The questions that must be asked include, then: at what point did it become generally accepted in Denmark that people were not individually responsible for being unemployed? Or alternatively: was this ever actually generally accepted by the Danish public? And closely related to this: what claims could be made on the public authorities, both national and local, for support?

The extent of unemployment also had consequences for those in work. A high level of unemployment reduced the chances of wage increases, especially before the introduction of unemployment insurance provided some protection against loss of income. It may even have led to decreases in pay in real terms, and may have had other effects such as increasing productivity among those in work and affecting both occupational and geographical mobility.

So how were these interrelated issues presented in the newspaper debate?

1.1. Concepts and definitions

The concept of "the unemployed" first appeared in the Danish language in the first half of the 19th century, and it became common usage in the second half of that century. In this book the ILO definition is used: "the unemployed" are defined as being people of working age who are without paid work and are not

---

[1] The results of this project have been published in Jensen (2006, 2007a, 2007b, 2008a, 2008b).

self-employed, and who have actively sought work or self-employment within a given period.[2]

"Debate" is defined in the broadest possible sense as anything which is aimed at influencing opinion. In addition to the core meaning of the word, then, as a more or less direct dialogue between two or more debaters, it is to be regarded here as encompassing newspaper editorials, background feature articles, reports of proceedings in both chambers of Parliament,[3] reports of political or occupational group meetings, cartoons, and advertisements of activities related to the unemployed.

1.2. An overview of Danish press history, and the selection of newspapers for the study

A full overview of the history of the Danish press is beyond the scope of this publication. The Danish-speaking reader is referred to a number of publications by the press historians Niels Thomsen (1972) and Jette Drachmann Søllinge (1989, 1994, 1999) and to their jointly written work *De danske aviser* (Danish Newspapers) (1988, 1889, 1991). However, it will be useful to present a short outline of general trends in the history of the conditions under which the press worked as a background to the analysis in this volume and to the selection of material used.

When Denmark was ruled by absolute monarchy the press was subject to censorship, the main aim being to restrict opportunities for political opposition. This meant that the vast majority of the few newspapers in existence generally steered clear of political issues, and were in any case essentially conservative and loyal to the throne. In the 1830s, however, an opposition press did gradually appear. It supported the idea of a free constitution, and the newspapers were each linked to one of the various groups of national liberal politicians.

The new Danish Constitution of 1849 allowed free political debate, and this heralded the launch of a huge variety of daily papers. More or less all of these papers were linked to political parties, and acted as their mouthpieces and campaign organs. Most of the already existing papers quickly declared their allegiance to the Conservative Party, and these were joined by new publications; but in their turn the Liberal Party (which had its roots among farmers who

---

[2] See ILO (2003).
[3] Until the amendment of the Constitution in 1953, the Danish Parliament consisted of two houses, the *Folketing* and the *Landsting*. Since 1953 there has been only one chamber, the *Folketing*.

supported free trade) and various factions of that party, the Social Democrats and the Social Liberal Party all established their own networks of newspapers across the country. The goal of each of the four parties was to control a newspaper in every town of any significance, resulting in what became known as "the four paper system". In addition, a number of essentially non-political popular papers were established in the larger towns, and especially in Copenhagen.

There has been a general gradual trend towards depoliticisation of the Danish press since the beginning of the 20th century. This trend began with the "press reform", which can be dated to the transformation of *Politiken* into a modern newspaper in 1905. From being more or less purely party mouthpieces, whose role was to recruit, instruct and mobilise voters by informing and persuading, Danish newspapers have gradually dropped their ties to political parties. This process was particularly marked in the wake of the closure of many newspapers after the Second World War, a period of newspaper extinction which meant that those remaining in existence were often the only papers serving a particular region. Such sole survivors were obliged to address themselves to a readership consisting of the entire population of the area, regardless of political opinion. The result has been that press coverage has become fairly neutral in its attitude towards particular political parties, and that expressions of opinion by the newspapers have taken on a less party-specific character.

Because the national newspapers have been the leading shapers of political opinion in Denmark, owing to their dominance in terms of circulation and editorial strength, this study is based primarily on the major national papers. In addition, the papers have been selected so as to represent the most important positions across the political spectrum of any given period. In the period before 1850, that political spectrum meant the "conservatives", who supported absolutism and were in opposition to the National Liberals and to the farmers' movements, which later gave rise to the Liberal Party.

After 1850 the analysis takes in the leading papers representing the Conservative, Liberal, Social Democrat (after 1871) and Social Liberal (after 1905) parties. Up until 1870 the National Liberal press is included, and from around 1910 the representatives of more revolutionary parties are taken into account: first the Syndicalist united opposition movement up until 1920, and since then the Danish Communist Party. The Socialist People's Party and a number of other parties have never been able to support their own press organs for a length of time or with a level of circulation sufficient to have had any real impact as part of the Danish media.

The selection of papers used in the analysis thus comprises, firstly, *Berlingske Tidende* (Conservative), *Social-Demokraten* (Social Democrat), *Politiken* (Social Liberal) and *Jyllands-Posten* (Conservative/Independent). Since the

Liberal Party has not been represented in the national press since 1905, and since their agrarian and moderate wings have never enjoyed such representation, a number of provincial papers that have been the most prominent mouthpieces for that party have also been included. In the early days after its foundation, *Fyns Tidende* was a leading Liberal organ, especially for the moderate wing of the party, and is therefore included. From the 1950s onward, *Fyns Tidende* is replaced in the analyses by *Vestkysten*, as this paper took over the role of the leading opinion-shaping Liberal paper.

Also included, though to a lesser extent, are *Solidaritet* (Syndicalist) and *Arbejderbladet/Land og Folk* (Communist), which are used mainly in connection with the newspaper debate during the last two years of the First World War; the inter-war period and during the Occupation, when revolutionary tendencies were widespread among the unemployed; and for periods when it might be expected that the unemployed could be a source of civil unrest. Similarly, limited use is made for the period 1937-45 of the newspaper of the Danish National Socialist Party, *Fædrelandet*.

In order to include opposition newspapers from the period before *Social-Demokraten* and *Politiken* were launched in 1872 and 1884 respectively, the Copenhagen papers *Fædrelandet* and *Kjøbenhavnsposten* have been included. Up until March 1848 *Fædrelandet* was the mouthpiece of the National Liberal opposition, and it continued to be the press organ of this political grouping in the newly-formed Parliament. *Kjøbenhavnsposten* put forward more revolutionary views during a short period in 1848. Neither of these papers concerned themselves to any great extent with farming issues, even though these affected most of the population; consequently, *Almuevennen* has been drawn on from time to time to fill that gap.

Since *Berlingske Tidende* has through most of its existence been a relatively moderate debate forum and has also appealed primarily to civil servants, it has been supplemented with the papers which most clearly represent commercial interests, *Dagens Nyheder/Nationaltidende*.

Appendix 2 presents a description of each individual newspaper, tracing its political allegiances over time and profiling its content and readership.

The book has another appendix (Appendix 1) which gives the results of a quantitative analysis of the number of items per year related to unemployment published in *Berlingske Tidende* and *Social-Demokraten/Aktuelt* throughout the 20th century. These data are compared with information about the unemployment cycle in order to examine the correlation between the intensity of the newspaper debate and levels of unemployment.

1.3. Translation of the newspaper titles

Approximated translations of the papers' titles are given in square brackets:

Aktuelt ["Current News"]

Almuevennen ["The Commoners' Friend"]

Arbejderbladet ["The Workers' Paper"]

Berlingske Tidende ["Berling's Times"]

Dagens Nyheder ["The Daily News"]

Fyns Tidende ["Funen's Times"]

Fædrelandet ["The Fatherland"]

Jyllands-Posten ["The Jutland Post"]

Kjøbenhavnsposten ["The Copenhagen Post"]

Land & Folk ["Country & People"]

Morgenavisen Jyllands-Posten ["The Morning Paper Jutland Post"]

Nationaltidende ["National Times"]

Nordjyden ["The North Jutlander"]

Politiken ["The Politics"]

Politiske Maanedsbreve ["Political Monthly Letters"]

Social-Demokraten ["The Social Democrat"]

Solidaritet ["Solidarity"]

Vestkysten ["The West Coast"]

References

Jensen, Bent. 2006. *Træk af avisdebatten om de arbejdsløse fra 1840'erne til 1940'erne. Volume I: Debatten indtil 1907.* Copenhagen: The Rockwool Foundation Research Unit.

Jensen, Bent. 2007a. *Træk af avisdebatten om de arbejdsløse fra 1840'erne til 1940'erne. Volume II: Debatten fra 1907 til 1940'erne.* Copenhagen: The Rockwool Foundation Research Unit.

Jensen, Bent. 2007b. "Et langt tilløb: Debatten om de arbejdsløse 1848-1907", in Jesper Hartvig Pedersen and Aage Huulgaard (eds) (2007). *Arbejdsløshedsforsikringsloven 1907-2007. Udvikling og perspektiver.* Copenhagen: Arbejdsdirektoratet.

Jensen, Bent. 2008a. *Træk af avisdebatten om de arbejdsløse fra 1950'erne til 1990'erne.* Odense: University Press of Southern Denmark.

Jensen, Bent. 2008b. *Hvad skrev aviserne om de arbejdsløse? Fra 1840'erne til 1990'erne.* Copenhagen: Gyldendal.

ILO. 2003. *Yearbook of Labour Statistics 2003.* Geneva: ILO.

Søllinge, Jette D. 1989. *Avistyper i Danmark fra begyndelsen i 1634 til i dag – en oversigt med vægten lagt på en typologisering efter indhold.* Paper presented at the 9th Nordic Conference for Mass Communication Research, Øland, 20-23 August 1989.

Søllinge, Jette D. 1994. Træk af udviklingen i dansk politisk journalistik 1900-1991. *Rotunden,* No. 3, 1994.

Søllinge, Jette D. 1999. Danish Newspapers. Structure and developments. *Nordicom Review,* Vol. 20, No. 1, 31-76.

Søllinge, Jette D. and Niels Thomsen. 1988, 1989 and 1991. *De danske aviser 1634-1989/91,* Volumes 1-3. Odense: Odense Universitetsforlag.

Thomsen, Niels. 1972. *Dagbladskonkurrencen 1870-1970: Politik, journalistik og økonomi i dansk dagpresses strukturudvikling.* Odense: Odense Universitetsforlag.

2. The Debate from 1848 to 1907

2.1. The prelude

In the 1830s the Danish debate on the unemployed was as yet very sporadic and largely focused on the concept of "lack of trade". The most significant contributions on this topic took widely differing views of the extent of the problem. In general, it was not seen as being an overwhelming problem in farming communities, but some contributors claimed that there was a widespread lack of trade among artisans in towns, the result of twenty years of unthinking revaluation of the currency. This created the first direct demand for the State to take action – a demand that there should be a loosening of the stringent monetary policy in order to create increased investment, with a resulting increase in economic activity. The assumption that there was widespread lack of trade among artisans was used by the liberals as an argument against absolutism.

Those forces who supported the status quo, in contrast, claimed that there was no significant problem of lack of trade, that the economy was expanding, and that this economic growth constantly created new needs, which in turn ensured increased demand. This was in effect a Danish version of Say's Law.[4] This did not mean, however, that the government should not initiate some economic reforms and abolish a number of limitations on commercial growth, for example by removing certain quite unreasonable taxes.

2.2. The debate in 1848, the European year of revolutions

The debate totally changed character in 1848. In the first place, the modern word "unemployment" came into widespread use, having first entered the Danish language around 1820. Secondly, unemployment came to be regarded from this point on as a part of the "labour question", and the left-leaning element of the Danish press, inspired by the revolutionary movement in Paris in the spring of 1848 and with *Kjøbenhavnsposten* in the forefront, put forward political demands that went far beyond questioning current monetary policy.

Among these demands were the setting in train of public works projects, to be carried out in National Workshops and using state financing; the introduction of free trade; and the establishment of a Ministry of Labour. There was a suggestion, dictated in part by the military campaign in Schleswig-Holstein but also partly inspired by developments in France, that the task of supplying the army and the fleet should be allocated to a number of different suppliers,

---

[4] Jean-Baptiste Say (1767-1832), a French economist, believed that supply created demand.

including firms controlled by the workers – though no such firms, it should be noted, were actually established in Copenhagen on this occasion. The proponents of this solution saw arming the unemployed as being the best guarantee for ensuring the power of the people. The workers themselves tried to solve the problem of unemployment in the spring of 1848 by driving German artisans out of Copenhagen. They were supported in their efforts by the city authorities, who were keen to see the capital rid of the German journeymen.

Almuevennen, the newspaper of the nascent farmers' movement, also expressed ideas about a right to social security, and the concept of the *right to work* turned up in background pieces about the situation in Paris in the spring of 1848. This paper's coverage of the topic, however, was far less sustained and systematic than that of the Copenhagen radical press.

Early in the spring of 1848 – i.e., before the abolition of absolutism in Denmark – there was a degree of sympathy expressed in National Liberal circles for the French revolution as well as for the French National Workshops and the guarantee of employment that they provided; but these views were completely reversed after the workers' bloody uprising in Paris in June 1848. After this, *Fædrelandet* warned time and time again against the inclusion of a right to work in the Danish constitution.

In this connection, the paper evolved an entire catalogue of arguments, both principled and practical, against the idea of the state having to guarantee work for all in every conceivable circumstance. One of the central points made was that a guarantee of employment would make workers lazy and involve the state in financial guarantees that would put fiscal pressures on the rest of the population. In its purest form, it was claimed, a declaration of rights would logically lead directly to socialism. In practice, it would only be in periods of economic decline that the state would face problems. However, a rather watered-down formulation was used in the Constitution of 1849, to the effect that those without the means of subsistence would be cared for by the public authorities. It was also accepted that the state would to a certain extent set in train or speed up various public works initiatives, just as had been proposed during the debate on the French constitution.

In the more popular elements of the conservative press, as in *Fædrelandet*, it was possible to detect a certain degree of sympathy for developments in France up until the June rising. After that point, however, these papers completely changed their standpoint. As far as the position at home was concerned, they warned against the political ferment among workers and argued for a strengthening of the police force.

The draft of the future Danish constitution was prepared in the autumn of 1848. Fædrelandet appears to have been pleased that there was nothing in the draft to suggest that the unemployed had a right to work; their view seems to have been based in part on the situation in Paris in 1848, where the right to work was viewed at one point as being almost an inalienable human right. Instead, the June Constitution of 1849 (pictured above) included a clause on the right to support from the public authorities for those who were not able to provide for themselves and their families. However, use of this right would lead to the loss of other civil rights, in particular the right to vote or to be elected. Photo: The Danish Royal Library.

In the main, comment on events in France in *Berlingske Tidende* followed the same pattern as that in *Fædrelandet* and the popular press. First there was a tone of expectant sympathy. This was followed by descriptions of the increasing difficulties faced by the provisional government and of the strain that the National Workshops placed on public finances and on commerce. Cheating and abuse became connected with the concept of state support to the unemployed.

In general, events in France – the establishment of National Workshops, the workers' uprising and the constitutional discussion on the right to work – contributed to a more careful consideration of the issue in Denmark, probably to a much greater extent than could be attributed to purely domestic problems of "the unemployed", and especially bearing in mind the low level of industrialisation in Denmark at that time. After 1848, any self-respecting National Liberal or Conservative would hold unequivocally that a constitutional right to work would lead directly to Socialism or Communism.

2.3. The 1850s and 1860s: An interlude

The debate on the unemployed continued throughout the 1850s and 1860s, becoming particularly topical during a crisis from 1857-59. Extremely high levels of unemployment (by modern standards) prevailing during the winters, combined with periods of high prices, also contributed to sustaining the debate. In the absence of an organised labour movement, the issue was raised primarily by associations which existed for philanthropic purposes, and by individual writers and politicians elected in Copenhagen. The focus was on the idea of "helping people to help themselves". Workers should be guided in solving their own problems through information and encouragement. Among the National Liberals, the prevailing theory was that liberalising the labour market through the removal of the restrictions in force during the time of absolute monarchy would in itself be the best means of fighting poverty and unemployment. One of the few protagonists in the debate to take a more socialist stance was Frederik Dreier, a doctor. He believed that unemployment could only be eliminated when industrial capitalism had been forced onto the defensive by manufacturing cooperatives owned by the workers themselves.

The non-socialist solutions proposed to ameliorate the problem included the establishment of a public labour directorate, to be run by a private company or by the Copenhagen municipal authority. A labour exchange of this kind would help the unemployed to help themselves. It would check that the unemployed really were available for the labour market and, provided that that was found to be the case, give either public help or support from the private charitable associations. This would avoid the paradoxical situation whereby firms sought in vain for labour, while there were workers who were being "pampered for their idleness".

In parallel with the proposal for a public labour exchange system, which did in fact operate for a while between June 1859 and April 1862, there were proposals – though not demands – for public works projects to be set in train during times of crisis. The unqualified demand for a universal citizens' right to work, as it was formulated in 1848, was not put forward again or debated in the newspapers.

In the newspapers' accounts of debates in Parliament around 1860, it is possible to identify a faction centred around the various liberal groupings which was against the state taking any initiative with respect to major public works in times of crisis. One argument was that the crisis itself should be allowed to resolve the situation, with workers being obliged to move to wherever there was work to be found. If the government created work in Copenhagen, this would only reinforce the trend for movement into the city from the countryside, and thus contribute to creating a potentially even greater unemployment problem. This became a standard viewpoint for a very long period into the future during the transformation of Denmark from an agricultural to an industrialised country, when the needs of industry for labour did not always coincide with the scale of migration to Copenhagen from the countryside.

Though they did not make reference to the self-regulating effects of crises, from 1864 the governing Conservative Party, dominated by the landed gentry, adopted a similar viewpoint.

Overall, then, there was little sympathy among the parliamentary parties for the idea that the state should take any responsibility for the unemployed through the initiation of public works projects, and any concept of general public responsibility for the unemployed was only hinted at on the very periphery of the debate. Neither the threat of revolution nor the collective strength of the working class exercised through the ballot box – only a minority of workers being enfranchised – could bring about such a policy orientation during the period between 1850 and 1870.

The general economic thinking in Denmark, which was predominantly shaped by economic theories developed in England and by Say's writings, considered that the industrial system was by and large in balance. Even though it was recognised that technological advances could lead to some problems of adjustment, it was thought that these problems would be reduced in proportion to the degree to which means of production and the related financial institutions were developed, and the extent to which the infrastructure enabled geographical mobility.

Major crises would only arise when industrialists increased their investment in fixed capital at the expense of circulating capital, i.e. when heavy investment in fixed assets temporarily reduced the amount of money available for spending on raw materials, labour, etc. Such crises, however, would simply be deviations from the general state of balance, and would usually be short-lived.

2.4. A Socialist agenda

The early 1870s saw the beginning of a new phase, with the establishment of a politicised workers' movement which gained a foothold in the immediate aftermath of the Paris Commune and which had clear international links: these Danish socialists were affiliated to the International Workingmen's Association (the First International).

During the economic boom at the beginning of the decade, the Socialists were most concerned with improving workers' wages through a series of strikes, which must also be viewed in the light of the fact that wages had fallen in real terms over several years during the 1860s. Around the middle of the decade Social-Demokraten began to follow the course of an incipient international economic crisis with some attention, and when the crisis broke in Denmark in 1876 the unemployed became an area of special focus and priority for the paper. Together with the trade union movement and the Social Democratic Party, the paper quickly established a position in support of demonstrations by the unemployed and of the demands that were made upon the government and Parliament when the Socialists in February 1877 called for the start of public works projects and for public welfare support for the unemployed, with no concomitant loss of their civil rights.

A completely new demand was for public grants to those of the unemployed who wished to emigrate and set up Socialist settlements in the USA. The argument in favour of emigration was influenced in part by Malthus' demographic theories, which also inspired the German socialist writer Lasalle, and in part by the practical experience in Britain and France of emigration as a remedy for unemployment. Once these settlements were established, it was argued, they could attract vast numbers of the unemployed and thus quite literally reduce the number of mouths to be fed from the resources of the domestic labour market.

The newspapers' coverage of discussions in both parliamentary chambers shows that the campaign of 1877 was a success, insofar as the ruling Conservative government bowed to pressure and passed a proposal through Parliament. This proposal made it possible for the municipalities to receive short-term state loans within a budget of one million kroner for use in small public works projects which would stimulate employment. A proposal from the Liberal Party to increase the budget by a further one million kroner to be given in direct grants to the municipalities, with the aim of strengthening the resources of the Poor Fund, was backed by a majority in the lower house, but was defeated in the upper

The Debate from 1848 to 1907   19

Illustreret Tidende (Illustrated News) showed in pictures the epic events taking place in Europe. The situation in Paris under the Commune is depicted above: "Insurgents keep watch in the Rue de la Paix and the Place Vendome in Paris" (16 April 1871). This scene showing the Parisian rebels was still peaceful. In the situation shown below, the Commune was finished and the score was to be settled (18 June 1871). Photo: The Danish Royal Library.

chamber by the Conservatives, who held a majority there as a result of the election rules.[5]

The Social Democrats had emphasised that they were making completely new demands of the Danish state in point of principle, and the debate and its effects took a new turn after 1877. In Denmark, the debate on state responsibility for the unemployed had previously been purely theoretical in nature, but now for the first time it had practical implications. On a more ideological note, the Social Democrats put forward the argument that unemployment would only disappear with the socialisation of the means of production, i.e. when worker-controlled cooperatives had taken over the factories and workshops. This would ensure a fair distribution of wealth in society and thus bring consumption capacity into line with production capacity of the industrial society.

The debate in Parliament revealed that the Liberals were opposed in principle to what was called "the active line", whereby the state would seek to ensure the availability of employment by subsidising public works projects. One reason for this was that they felt that state public works projects would interfere with "natural development", i.e. that they would prevent economic downturns from depressing wages. Perhaps the proposal also smelled rather too much of Socialism for the Liberals and was seen by them as establishing a dangerous precedent, just as French politicians had foreseen in 1848 that a state obligation to ensure the provision of employment for all workers would lead directly to Socialism. It was also felt that it would increase the economic dominance of the larger towns over rural areas. Despite these misgivings, however, the Liberals gave way and aligned themselves with the proposal, given the severity of the situation.

The Conservatives took the pragmatic view that the state would get something back for the outlay of public funds, while the alternative "support line" might lead to passivity among the unemployed; making the unemployed self-supporting was always to be preferred to giving them handouts. The state would in fact only be making loans to the municipalities, thus ensuring that the involvement of the state in the matter would be unchanged in principle; care for the poor would remain completely in the hands of the municipal authorities and the Independent Poor Funds. The Conservatives generally believed that the problem in the capital would be significantly reduced if only the government could initiate some major public spending projects of a military nature. This idea was rejected by both the Liberals and the Social Democrats; in the case of the latter, not only were they generally pacifist in their outlook, but they also believed that rapid rearmament would actually make unemployment worse,

---

[5] Of the 66 members of the upper house, 12 were selected by the monarch and served for life. Half of the rest were chosen by and from among the wealthiest 3% of voters (Thomsen (1979), p. 22).

since it would require increased taxation, which would dampen activity in the private sector.

The issue of taxation methods was also raised in the course of the political skirmishing over unemployment. The Liberals, who wanted a tax reform centred on direct taxation, attacked the Conservatives' emphasis on indirect taxation, which was socially inequitable and reduced the disposable income and thus the consumption of the average citizen. In addition, according to the Liberals, the Conservatives hoarded money in the Treasury, thus further depressing levels of consumption. In this way, the unemployed – like every other conceivable political issue in this period – became deeply embroiled in the long conflict between Conservatives and Liberals.

After the middle of the 1870s it was the Social Democrats who set the agenda for the political debate on the unemployed, but the parliamentary political parties were never able to deal with the issue of unemployment outside the context of the great political conflict between the Liberals and the Conservatives. The two leading parliamentary groups, with the Liberals having a majority in the lower house and the Conservatives in the upper, were locked in a battle to shape Danish democracy which continued unabated until 1901. There was nothing in the most recent version of the Constitution, that of 1866, about how conflicts between the upper and lower houses of parliament should be resolved; and the situation was in no way helped by the fact that both houses had to pass proposed legislation before it could become law. This lack of clarity, and the fact that the upper house was markedly more conservative in character than the lower, signalled the start of the long political conflict that later became known as the Constitutional Struggle.

As the years went by this conflict intensified, effectively blocking most parliamentary initiatives. A series of proposals for dispensations from the law concerning the Poor Fund or state grants via the municipalities to the Poor Fund thus all stalled in Parliament, with one very limited exception, as a result of the internal conflict which effectively paralysed all legislative work in Denmark.

The Social Democrats were represented in the lower house from 1884 onwards, and used their parliamentary platform to promote proposals for assisting the unemployed. One new initiative was a proposal in 1886 for an increased state loan to the Municipality of Copenhagen that would have enabled much-needed urban renewal work to be carried out. This would naturally also have had a significant job-creation effect. The proposal was promoted in cooperation with Herman Trier, a Social Liberal member of the Liberal group; with "the unemployed" as a central issue, this consolidated the recently initiated collaboration between Social Liberal forces among the Liberals and the Social Democrats. This cooperation was to point the way forward to the formation of a strong political block that was to persist until the end of the First World War, thus underlining the importance that the unemployment issue had for the workers. At the same time, we can see how the arguments formulated concerning the unemployed and the demand for state assistance for them were used to spearhead the Social Democrats' attempts to extend the role of the state in society. If the workers gained a foothold in Parliament, suggested *Social-Demokraten*, they would certainly manage in the future to achieve a redistribution of the wealth of society.

In every year from the end of the 1870s onward, the initiatives proposed by the Social Democrats to help the unemployed were legion. There were proposals for the introduction of an 8-hour working day for those in municipal employment, proposals for the support for worker-controlled manufacturing cooperatives, demands for public works projects, demands to waive claims for repayment of financial assistance received by the poor in times of crisis, and demands to maintain the purchasing power of workers' wages.

At the same time, it was emphasised again and again in *Social-Demokraten* that the problem of unemployment would only disappear for good when the means of production had been socialised. However, the period saw a shift in the theoretical basis of the Social Democrats' beliefs from Lasalle to Marx, from manufacturing cooperatives to state control of the means of production – though without this necessarily entailing the adoption of pure Marxist revolutionary theory. The Social Democrats were increasingly inclined towards the idea of a gradual and peaceful transformation of society, with democracy as a prerequisite for socialism. With society controlling the means of production, manufacturing would be released from the grasp of speculators, and a completely new pattern of distribution of income in society would mean that the consumption capacity of the country would match its ever increasing production capacity.

However, no major initiatives were actually taken by the state. It is a matter for debate whether this was primarily due to the Liberals' obstruction of the landowner-dominated government, or to a series of internal splits in the Liberal Party, or to the struggle by the Conservatives against the dominant position of the lower house in Parliament. It is also debatable whether Denmark was really so much later with state intervention than many other European nations, with Germany as a notable exception. Whatever the answers to these questions, it was not until the 1890s that progress was made in the field of social legislation; however, the initatives did not yet comprise attempts towards unemployment.

2.5. The debate in the 1880s and 1890s

In the absence of any major public initiatives over and above the established systems for support of the poor, including the aid provided by the Poor Fund, private generosity continued to be of great importance in supporting the "worthy" unemployed during periods of extreme shortage of work. The underlying concept continued to be that of helping people to help themselves, which resulted in strict checks of the worthiness of the recipients.

In terms of amounts, private donations were still the dominant source of funds in the 1880s in comparison with the sums collected by the trade unions. However, towards the middle of the 1880s it became apparent that the trade union movement had developed an organisation that would make it possible to collect significant amounts of money. At the same time, the trade union movement was becoming organised in a way that allowed a larger number of trade unions to undertake a more comprehensive degree of responsibility for the support of the unemployed. Politically, this was expressed in the form of proposals for legislation concerning recognised unemployment funds, which the Social Democrats put forward repeatedly from the parliamentary session of 1896-97 onward, with exhaustive coverage in *Social-Demokraten*.

According to *Social-Demokraten*, the argument of the workers' party was that unemployment was the greatest social problem of the age, and that it was set down in the Constitution that the state had an obligation to help those who could not support themselves. Unemployment was society's problem, the paper stated, and an individual bore no personal responsibility for being unemployed. *Social-Demokraten* also emphasised that the proposal ensured that only the involuntarily unemployed would be entitled to support; the Minister for Home Affairs was also to be guaranteed the right to check the operation of the Funds thoroughly in order to control that unemployment funds were not used as strike funds. In other words, the proposal was intended to be neutral in the social struggle between workers and employers.

According to the coverage in the right-of-centre press, the Minister for Home Affairs regarded the proposal as embodying the Communist principle that the State should guarantee the right to work for all. The state-recognised unemployment funds would in reality also strengthen the unions in their provision of strike funds. Giving support exclusively to manual workers who were union members would be socially unjust. Furthermore, the papers argued, state support could create incentive problems, and there was a risk that unemployment might end up being self-inflicted as a result of unrealistic wage demands.

2.6. A breakthrough

With the change in the system of government in 1901, when it became parliamentary practice that a government had to have the support of a majority in the lower house or *Folketing*, the Liberals came into power. This gave the Social Democrats and the trade unions every reason to press even harder for the introduction of recognised unemployment funds.

Help from the State for the unemployed, channelled through the trade unions, would relieve pressure on wages during periods of recession, and the loss of membership of the unions would be reduced, argued *Social-Demokraten*. In periods of economic growth, the existence of unemployment funds would be an incentive for individual workers to join a union.

Among economists, the increasing interest in the "worker question" in the 1890s combined with the increasing level of industrialisation led to a detailed discussion of the experience of other countries with the use of unemployment statistics, and consequently to an implicit demand for equivalent statistics for Denmark.

Opinions were divided over the question of unemployment insurance, as they also were over the idea of obligatory saving. Those who favoured obligatory saving schemes claimed that this would inhibit problems of abuse and at the same time create a more peaceable labour market. The opponents saw the shadow of a police state lurking behind the pages of the savings books.

The parliamentary session of 1902-03 saw a breakthrough for the supporters of recognised unemployment funds. The Conservatives now also put forward a proposal for state support of unemployment funds, provided that their finances were kept completely separate from those of the trade unions. Legislation on recognised unemployment funds seemed certain to be passed by Parliament in the not-too-distant future.

References

Thomsen, Niels. 1979. *Historiske opinionsstudier med et eksempel fra provisorietiden*. Copenhagen: Folkeuniversitetet.

3. The debate from the first law on state-recognised unemployment funds in 1907 until the 1940s

3.1. The climate of opinion at the time of the adoption of the law

It is apparent from an examination of the character of the debate in 1906/07 that there was general political unanimity regarding the necessity for legislation on unemployment funds. Unemployment was a recurring phenomenon, and the legislature now recognised that the economy was subject to cycles that resulted in periods of increased unemployment. There was therefore general agreement that the state should step in to support voluntary insurance schemes in accordance with the "Ghent" system, whereby unemployment insurance is voluntary, and if not formally in practice, it is administered by trade unions.[6] According to *Social-Demokraten*, this system would provide an education in democratic socialism, while at the same time there was no doubt that the existence of unemployment funds, of which half of the total costs of the fund was covered by the public purse, would promote the unionisation of the workers.

There were differences on various points, however. First, the Social Democrats demanded that the unions and the unemployment funds be directly linked in their organisation. This opinion was supported in part by the Social Liberals. One possible explanation for this unanimity was the existence of an alliance between the two parties, ostensibly developed for the purpose of overthrowing the government, but which in fact had its roots going back to the 1880s.

On the opposite side of the argument were the Conservatives and the Liberals, who argued for a clear division between the unemployment funds and the unions, so that the money in the funds could not be used in support of labour market conflicts. This argument was based in part on the view that trade unions were partisan organisations, and as such should not be eligible for support from the state. Further, the two parties advanced the argument that the state also had an obligation to support workers who were not part of the trade union movement, and that such workers would not be able to benefit if the unions had direct control over the unemployment insurance funds.

A second area of disagreement lay in the evaluation of the possible incentive effects of unemployment funds. The Liberals emphasised the importance of designing checking arrangements to prevent abuse of the system. At the opposite end of the political spectrum, the Social Democrats believed that the process of checking should not be so stringent that workers were forced to take work at a wage that was below that current for their skills. The rules should also not be formulated in such a way that they were an insult to the dignity of the workers.

---

[6] The development of the Ghent system in Denmark is described in Danish in Pedersen and Huulgaard (2007); see also Vater (ed.) (1932).

In 1908, at a point when a serious crisis in private house-building had developed in Copenhagen, an opposition group to the left of the Social Democrats began to make an impression. This Syndicalist opposition immediately recognised the unemployed as a significant group that could be mobilised. For the entire remainder of the century, the Social Democrats always felt threatened by the possibility that an opposition grouping to the left of them would grow in strength during long periods of widespread unemployment.

A drawing published in Social-Demokraten of a meeting of the unemployed in the spring of 1908 (16 April 1908). Photo: The Danish Royal Library.

From the coverage in the other newspapers it can be seen that there was, as in 1906/07 before the passing of the legislation on recognised unemployment funds, widespread agreement that it was up to the State to take the initiative and help the unemployed by speeding up the introduction of public spending projects and extending the frame of reference for unemployment funds and other welfare funds at times of acute crisis. Plans were thus made for a two-pronged strategy built on use of the unemployment funds during periods of normal unemployment and additional support via the welfare funds for continued help to those whose right to unemployment benefit had expired during periods of extraordinarily high unemployment. Within two years of the passing of the law, around 60% of male industrial workers and just under 20% of female workers in industry had enrolled in one of the recognised unemployment funds.

3.2. The debate during the First World War

During the First World War, both the State and the various organisations had a major role to play in keeping conditions as normal as possible for production and consumption – and for the life of society in general. However, with low levels of unemployment from the spring of 1915 until the autumn of 1917, the unemployment funds were not among the most important actors in this regulation of the nation's affairs, and similarly the unemployed were not a topic that concerned the newspapers overmuch. This situation changed, however, when unemployment shot up in the autumn of 1917 as a result of the supply problems created by the all-out submarine warfare in the North Sea. The Danish Syndicalists – whose influence had been extremely modest during the first years of the war – now sought to mobilise the unemployed, who were not only out of work but also suffering as a result of the high prices and shortages that marked the entire war-time period, despite state-imposed maximum prices and rationing.

In October 1917 the government and Parliament were already trying to limit the social consequences of the rising level of unemployment through extraordinary legislation that strengthened the support provided in step with the growing shortages, and also allowed new groups to obtain help from the funds. Nevertheless, it is apparent from the newspapers that around mid-December 1917 there was a high level of activity among the unemployed in Copenhagen and the larger towns, and that some activity was also noticeable in small market towns. The rhetoric at the meetings of the unemployed was influenced by the Syndicalist organisation of the movement, and the unemployed became an ever more clearly defined and articulate grouping in the life of the capital and the large towns.

Social-Demokraten chose at first to attempt a metaphorical enveloping of the movement. The party newspaper aligned itself with the call by the unemployed for reform and covered their activities closely, but at the same time never gave the Syndicalist organisers any space in their columns. In parallel with publishing information about the initiatives that came from the unemployed themselves, the paper printed full accounts of the comprehensive range of activities intended to promote the interests of the unemployed carried out by the Social Democratic Party, the trade union movement, the Social Liberal government and, in particular, the Social Democrat-led municipalities.

This was in a way a rather dangerous double game, since it was clearly stated for all to see in the Syndicalist paper *Solidaritet* that the Syndicalists were actually the driving force behind the workers' movement. Further, the right-of-centre papers emphasised the fact that leading Social Democrats participated in the demonstration by the unemployed at the beginning of January 1918, despite the fact that it was organised and controlled by the Syndicalists.

When the Syndicalists stepped up their criticism of the Social Democrats, and with new legislation almost in place towards the end of January, *Social-Demokraten* showed its true colours at last. The claims of the unemployed had indeed been formulated by the Syndicalist opposition, but the Social Democrats and the trade union movement had tried to restrain the workers and direct them towards making their demands in Parliament. They had discouraged the workers from actions of a criminal nature that could rebound against all the unemployed and against the workers' movement itself. Now the Social Democrat leaders had no choice but to distance themselves from the revolutionary activists among the unemployed, and the paper's criticism of the Syndicalists became from this point onward couched in much more direct terms, sharing in the same rhetoric of hatred that their opponents had been using for a long time.

It is possible to see an acknowledgement of this distancing by the Social Democrat leadership in the right-of-centre papers. There was general acceptance of the need to strengthen the unemployment funds and raise the level of support they provided, in part because of the impact of rising unemployment and of increasing shortages, and in part – though this was less openly acknowledged – because of the threat inherent in the radicalisation of the unemployed and the revolutionary movements in Europe. This acceptance, however, was not so complete that the right-of-centre papers could refrain from pointing out the "moral problems" that would arise from an over-generous level of support – diminished appetite for work and increased idleness.

The Social Liberal *Politiken* quoted the Social Liberal Minister for Home Affairs as saying that the level of unemployment benefit might in certain cases reach the level of the minimum wage. But it was not the level of benefit that was the problem: it was the low wages. In general, it is clear from the coverage of the unemployment problem in *Politiken* and *Social-Demokraten* that the parties which these papers represented were in close harmony on the whole issue during the winter of 1917-18, including their views on the level of unemployment benefit and initiatives to be taken concerning the unemployed.

The winter of 1917-18 saw many of the unemployed taking direct action under the influence of the Syndicalists. The picture above shows one such demonstration, and below can be seen the deputation sent in to Parliament by the unemployed (Social-Demokraten, 10 January 1918). Photo: The Danish Royal Library.

The agitation by the Syndicalists was typically directed just as much against the Social Democrats as it was against "the capitalist class enemy". Typically, too, the Syndicalists attempted to mobilise the unemployed and thereby pressure the Social Democrats into more radical action. Ultimately, it was the aim of the Syndicalists to use the unemployed workers' movement as part of a revolutionary uprising, though it was far from clear what kind of social structure they wanted to have as a replacement for the existing one.

The intrusion in February 1918 by the unemployed into the Copenhagen Stock Exchange, accompanied by physical assaults on the stockbrokers – "The Storming of the Exchange" – marked the climax of the actions by the unemployed that were organised by the Syndicalists in the winter of 1917-18. The episode was, however, very limited in its extent, probably in part because the parties in Parliament had just reached agreement on revised legislation which provided for additional help to the unemployed. This meant that the significant emergency assistance introduced in the autumn of 1917 would be continued and expanded. With very few exceptions, the press characterised the Syndicalists' action as a flop. The larger papers were in agreement that only a limited number of the demonstrators had actually been members of the unemployed. In fact, the demonstrators were largely young hooligans who had been manipulated by a small number of fanatical Syndicalist leaders, they claimed. Only *Solidaritet* maintained that it was the unemployed acting as a united force that were involved, and that the revolutionary power of this group remained intact after the action.

The larger newspapers described the Syndicalists as cowards of a criminal disposition. *Social-Demokraten* added its opinion that they were divisive trouble-makers. When the right-of-centre press discussed this group, it was – according to *Social-Demokraten* – with the thinly veiled agenda of preventing the working class from negotiating politically during times of shortages and widespread unemployment through a strong Social Democratic Party and a united trade union movement.

According to *Social-Demokraten*, the actions were in fact being used by the Conservatives as an argument to throw out the Social Liberal government, which was supported by the Social Democrats. The Social Democrats were thus being squeezed from two sides: by the political right, who wanted to get rid of the Social Democrat-supported government, and by the Syndicalists, who wanted to mobilise the workers in a revolutionary movement. In retrospect, however, it is clear that the right was being relatively restrained over the question of the unemployed during the last year of the war, for fear that they might provoke social unrest.

The Storming of the Exchange was front page news in Politiken of 12 February 1918. The event was not interpreted as a revolutionary uprising, however. The paper simply wrote of "a disorderly day in the history of Copenhagen". Photo: The Danish Royal Library.

In the course of the spring of 1918 the level of unemployment dropped to about half that of the preceding winter, and consequently the issue of unemployment became much less significant for the agitation of the Syndicalists. Instead they threw themselves – with a considerable degree of success – into struggles in the workplace for increased wages and for the reduction of the working day to eight hours. At the same time, the Syndicalists were active in helping conscientious objectors and in fermenting agitation among the soldiers in the armed forces. When the Syndicalist disturbances reached a new and greater climax with violent rioting in Copenhagen in November 1918, the unemployed were not the focus of their activity.

With revolutionary activities going on just to the south of the Danish border, the government and civil authorities were considerably more concerned on this occasion than they had been in February 1918. However, once again no revolution broke out in Denmark, and with the improved economic conditions in 1919 it was possible to abolish the many special war-time regulations that had been in force, including the emergency legislation on unemployment funds. The right-of-centre papers had got their teeth into "the moral problem": the allegedly high level of unemployment benefit undermined "the will to work". The politicians of the right wanted to return to the fundamental idea of the unemployment funds, i.e. of helping people to help themselves, on the basis of a philosophy of insurance against bad times and with strict and effective controls. In connection with the Syndicalist-organised workers' struggle, the right-wing politicians also wished to withdraw benefits from any of the unemployed who refused to take work in a firm that was the target of an illegal, i.e. unofficial strike.

3.3. The debate in the 1920s

It appears from the reports in *Social-Demokraten* on the conference of unemployment funds in 1919 that a wish was also expressed there for stricter checks in order to avoid abuse of unemployment benefits, despite the fact that the paper had initially explicitly denied that there was any such problem. It is also apparent that the funds were looking to increase the membership subscriptions in a move towards a return to the principles of their origins in 1907. Conditions seemed favourable for a normalisation of the labour market, with something approaching full employment. Many were hoping that Denmark could return to the general economic climate prevailing before the war.

The war had brought distortions into the legislation on unemployment funds, the original philosophical basis of the 1907 Act of Parliament having been one of helping workers to help themselves through a system that was primarily insurance based. At the same time, checking up on the unemployed had become administratively impossible towards the end of the war, when access to the funds had been opened up to an entirely new group of claimants. Under pressure from Syndicalist-led workers, benefit levels had also been raised in order to compensate for the high prices caused by war-time shortages – a problem that was in fact relieved by a period of deflation throughout the 1920s.

Against this background, the debate on the unemployed in the 1920s can be viewed as a trial of strength between a weakened workers' movement on the one hand and the new governments of the Liberals, and their conservative parliamentary basis, who were in power for most of the decade, on the other.

The right-of-centre papers all interpreted the arguments about the unemployed in the same way at both the beginning and the end of the 1920s. They claimed that the more widely available benefits undermined the will to work. The unemployment funds were available for use by the trade union movement as state-subsidised strike funds, contributing to a wave of major and minor strikes. The resulting wage increases, they stated, were not matched by productivity, and this in fact exacerbated unemployment.

This view was completely in line with the changes in economic thinking at the end of the 19th century, when economists had stated their belief that trade unionism was an anomaly in a free market that could, through the creation of a monopoly in the production factor labour, increase unemployment. The Liberals and the Conservatives were divided on one point, however, namely the use of import duties as a weapon against unemployment. The free-trade oriented farmers were adamant in their opposition to this idea, while the Conservatives argued for the protection of industry in order to create more jobs in the cities.

Social-Demokraten argued that the Liberals were carrying out a policy of cutbacks that was damaging to society and in the interests of the large landowners and industrialists. The rhetoric of the class struggle was even more in evidence than in the pre-war period. On a more theoretical level, the paper argued – as ever – that reductions in the purchasing power of the population would intensify the crisis through a reduction in consumption. Finally, the paper pointed to the threat that the workers would cease to respect existing labour market agreements if they found that the State was collaborating in depressing wages through revision of the unemployment legislation. When the final negotiations on legislation began in the spring of 1927, the Social Democrats opted to boycott the process altogether. The result was a relatively comprehensive reduction in the benefits available under unemployment legislation, especially the abandoning of the extraordinary welfare benefits for long term unemployed. The stage was thus set for a revision of the law when the Social Democrats and the Social Liberals formed a coalition government in 1929.

3.4. The debate during the Great Depression

The international economic crisis affected Denmark remarkably little for most of 1930, but in the autumn of that year it did begin to have a really serious impact. The debate in the newspapers turned once more to the issue of the unemployed as the number of jobless rose.

The first presentation of a proposal for a thoroughgoing social reform by K.K. Steincke, the Social Democrat Minister for Social Affairs in the Social Democrat and Social Liberal coalition government established in 1929, set off a debate which showed that there was certainly awareness of the problem of unemployment, but that there was still some doubt as to how serious the crisis would turn out to be.

The disagreement over the need for social reform was especially marked between the Social Democrats and Social Liberals on the one hand and the Liberals on the other, the latter remaining solidly behind the *laissez-faire* principles of the 1920s. The Social Democrats argued that the workers would gradually cover the increased costs of social welfare themselves through the social insurance contributions and taxes that they paid, and the Social Affairs Minister also insisted that a reasonable level of support for the unemployed would help to counteract trends towards totalitarianism.

Levels of unemployment were high during the spring of 1931, and the Danish Communist Party began organising the unemployed. Their success took the nation's leaders by surprise, and it became harder for the four old parties and their newspapers to ignore their activities. During the riots of the spring of 1931 the Communist Party clearly demonstrated the potential for social conflict that existed among the unemployed. Nevertheless, the newspapers of the four old parties once again refused to admit that the disorder had its basis in the comprehensive organisation of the unemployed by the Communists.

Social-Demokraten once more trotted out the by now well-worn argument that the primary aim of the radical left was to create disunity among the working class and curb the influence of the Social Democrats. *Jyllands-Posten*, in contrast, claimed that it was in fact the consequences of Social Democrat policies that were now making themselves felt. Ruinous taxes were crippling business, and the vastly overgenerous social welfare benefits were encouraging ever increasing demands for higher levels of benefit and a general refusal to work. *Fyns Tidende* echoed the farmers' old cry from the heart: it was hard to understand how there could be unemployed workers standing around in the cities at the same time as agriculture sought in vain for labour. The familiar battle-lines of the 1920s between the Social Democrats and the Liberals thus remained in place during the first two years of the Depression.

By October 1931 the effects of the crisis had become so painful that both the Social Democrats and the Conservatives were ready for a first attempt at a compromise to alleviate the problems, modest though this proposal was. With the unemployed as a lever, the Social Democrats had succeeded in splitting the two major right-wing parties and thus in temporarily restoring the extraordinary welfare benefits. *Berlingske Tidende* had a tricky task in explaining this turn of events, while *Jyllands-Posten* and *Dagens Nyheder* were free to indulge in outpourings of editorial criticism of the Conservative Party leadership. The two papers claimed that the Conservatives had surrendered to the Social Democrats unconditionally, obtaining no substantial benefits for urban business interests in exchange.

However, by the summer of 1932 the crisis was biting even deeper, and the four old parties came together in a compromise that significantly strengthened the legislation on unemployment. It was hoped that this would contribute to undermining the Communist mobilisation of the unemployed. It was easy enough for *Social-Demokraten* and *Politiken* to endorse this compromise; both papers noted the significant improvement that was achieved in the conditions of the unemployed.

Fyns Tidende placed emphasis on the results achieved for agriculture, and in its interpretation of the implications of the compromise for unemployment legislation the paper pointed out that the insurance principle had been strengthened through the establishment of continuation funds, from which the workers could obtain continued assistance after the suspension of ordinary unemployment benefits.

In January 1933, when the "Kanslergade compromise" was agreed by the Social Democrats, the Social Liberals and the Liberals, we find the government-supporting *Social-Demokraten* arguing strongly in favour of emergency work programmes and social reforms. In general, the paper maintained the importance of a state that actively regulated and controlled society, arguing that social reform – now to be implemented – was a significant step forward in this connection and that the Kanslergade compromise had now prepared the way for such social reform. At the same time, the newspaper pointed out that the reform was so tightly drawn up that it would not artificially increase the number of unemployed by removing the motivation to work. In many respects, the coverage by *Politiken* echoed that of *Social-Demokraten*. The paper also prioritised the need for active government management of the crisis of the 1930s, in part through public works projects that would provide employment. The importance of a coherent and transparent social policy in the shape of Steincke's reform was also recognised.

In *Fyns Tidende*, organ of the Liberal Party, we can observe a clear shift in the perspective of the social affairs commentary and the views regarding the unemployed before and after the compromise. Before the agreement, the paper published a number of articles that linked the significant extension in the Danish social legislation with a trend towards increased problems of incentives to work. The will of the unemployed to help themselves was being degraded, the paper claimed, as evidenced by the increase in the numbers on poor relief. After the agreement, the angle shifted; now it was emphasised that thanks to the input from the Liberals, the social reform was sufficiently strict in nature. Furthermore, claimed the paper, the compromise agreement that winter to manage the crisis had paved the way for an upturn in the economy, which was the most important thing.

The Conservatives did not participate in the winter crisis agreement, and consequently it is not surprising that the most critical reactions to it were to be found in the pages of *Berlingske Tidende* and *Dagens Nyheder*. *Berlingske Tidende*, for example, never missed an opportunity to highlight connections between the new social legislation and what the paper regarded as rapidly spiralling taxes. The two papers also sought to demonstrate major work incentive problems. As a result of the new social legislation, declared *Berlingske Tidende*, many Danish citizens would prefer to live on state benefits rather than work, and to back up this assertion the paper included a number of reports from the provinces of the unemployed carousing in the evenings with the benefit money they received from the municipalities during the daytime.

In its cartoons, too, Social-Demokraten stressed that what the workers wanted most, was work. "Spring is the season of hope, they say – and it would be true enough if you happened to be a tree". Drawing by Anton Hansen in Social-Demokraten, 2 April 1933. Photo: The Danish Royal Library.

The Communist paper *Arbejderbladet*, on the other hand, regarded the social reform as a capitalist expedient that would not allow the workers any socio-political concessions.

The economic situation improved somewhat after 1933, even though unemployment figures remained very high, especially for unskilled workers. Now the will to compromise became less evident, and indeed as a result of the government gaining a majority in the upper house – Landstinget – in 1936, less important; and there was a return to the old familiar positions. The climate of ideological debate from the end of the 1920s was thus re-established until war came to Denmark in the April of 1940.

The new element in the Social Democrat argumentation in the 1930s was the idea that an effective welfare benefit and employment creation policy could prevent the unemployed from succumbing to the lure of Fascism.

3.5. Occupation and Liberation

During the wartime German occupation of Denmark public debate on the unemployed, as on most issues, was hampered by conditions of censorship and restriction; and the fact that the four old parties were united in a coalition government from April 1940 until August 1943 also reduced the potential for disagreement. This situation is reflected in the newspaper articles published during the occupation. In general, the parties took a middle line in their views, with a softening of the old strong ideological views on support for and checks on the unemployed.

This was clearly expressed in the debaters' views of the benefit to society of the government initiating employment-creation projects in order to resolve the problem of unemployment. All the papers adopted a positive stance on the issue.

The points that were never mentioned, but which undoubtedly underlay the positive opinions expressed in, for example, *Berlingske Tidende*, were the threat of forced shipment of labour to Germany in the event of high unemployment and the fear that the unemployed could be mobilised by either the Communists or the Danish Nazis. In the legal press, however, there were only a few hints of activism among the unemployed, and in comparison with the 1930s protests by the unemployed were very weak.

The only paper that persistently failed to support the consensus was the National Socialist *Fædrelandet*, which consistently deplored what it described as temporary solutions to paper over the cracks. Only a complete change in the system could banish unemployment for good and bring the Danish workers into an employment situation that was worthy of the nation.

In the first years of the occupation, the democratic newspapers were neutral to vaguely positive towards the idea of Danes working in Germany. But there were only a limited number of articles on the topic recorded in the papers, though again with the exception of *Fædrelandet*, which not surprisingly was very positive regarding this employment opportunity for Danish workers. In contrast, the underground Communist press attacked at regular intervals the export of the unemployed to aid the Nazi war economy. The Communists claimed that every Dane in Germany freed up a German to fight in Hitler's war, to the detriment of the Danish cause. The Communist press also named and openly attacked politicians in the government who it claimed had totally capitulated to the German demands in this context.

As the end of the war approached, the unemployed were given more attention in the papers, and it became evident that among both politicians and the general public there was a strong determination to avoid a crisis such as that which followed the First World War. The public authorities, with the full approval of the politicians, built up a list of public works projects that would provide employment and which could be set in train as soon as the necessary materials were available. At the same time, the politicians encouraged the business community to take its share of responsibility for maintaining the workforce in employment.

The Communist paper *Land og Folk* attempted to raise the workers in connection with demands for full compensation in the event of enforced work-sharing or unemployment, and in March 1945 the civil service issued certain regulations, with the knowledge and agreement of the politicians of the old parties, which went a considerable way towards meeting these demands on a number of important points. The Communists also attempted to have full employment included in the programme of the liberation government. Formally, this demand was not met, but the subject of full employment and full compensation in the event of unemployment or work-sharing did form a part of the government's accession declaration in May 1945 – a declaration that received intensive coverage in all the newspapers included in this survey.

The demand for full employment was echoed in the conferences of the labour unions, and from the USA and the UK came reports that full employment had indeed been achieved. In Sweden, too, there were positive signals with respect to employment.

Could Denmark also escape from the chronic unemployment problem that had beset the country through the twenties, thirties and part of the occupation?

Full employment was the concern of all sectors of society, claimed Berlingske Tidende at the beginning of 1945. On 7 January 1945 the paper published an opinion poll on the extent to which the public believed full employment to be a realistic goal after the war. "Many believe that unemployment can be avoided after the war", read the headline. Photo: The Danish Royal Library.

References

Pedersen, Jesper Hartvig and Aage Huulgaard (eds). (2007). *Arbejdsløshedsforsikringsloven 1907-2007. Udvikling og perspektiver.* Copenhagen: Arbejdsdirektoratet.

Vater, Aage (ed.). (1932). *Arbejdsløshedsforsikringsloven i Danmark gennem 25 Aar 1907-1932.* Copenhagen: Direktoratet for Arbejdsanvisningen og Arbejdsløshedsforsikringen.

4. The period from 1950 to the mid-1990s

4.1. The early 1950s

In the period immediately after liberation, there was a strong feeling among the general public that it was the responsibility of the government and the business community to guarantee full employment – which was fully in line with the views held in other Western European countries in 1945. The peoples of Europe were not prepared under any circumstances to return to the mass unemployment and social unrest of the 1930s, and from 1947 to 1950 the Danish Social Democrat government insisted on maintaining full employment. However, the government fell in the autumn of 1950 after losing a vote in the *Folketing* concerning the removal of the some of the last elements of war-time rationing.

A coalition government of the Liberals and Conservatives was installed. At first there was little discussion of the theme of unemployment in the newspapers, but from the spring of 1951 articles concerning the unemployed and the rising level of unemployment appeared in ever-increasing numbers in the pages of *Social-Demokraten* as an argument against the government and their economic policies. The government was using a credit squeeze in its attempt to stabilise the Danish balance of payments, which was under constant threat. As the former Prime Minister H.C. Hansen expressed during the debate in Parliament on the budget in October 1951, "The Social Democrats will never accept a policy that uses unemployment as a means to solve Denmark's exchange and economic problems."

Similarly, *Social-Demokraten* argued that permitting unemployment to rise was not an appropriate means of solving the country's problems. Neither unemployment nor the fear of unemployment would increase productivity, argued the paper, and a lower level of production worsened Denmark's foreign trade position. Furthermore, the increased defence costs that resulted from Danish membership of NATO would be harder to bear when production was below optimal.

Social-Demokraten demanded that the current government economic policy be replaced with an industrial policy based on state coordination of investment and production.

In contrast, the right-of-centre politicians – as reported in *Berlingske Tidende*, *Jyllands-Posten* and *Vestkysten* – insisted that the government economic policy was a sound response to the need to protect the currency during a necessary process of liberalisation of foreign trade. The government would have preferred to use a regulation index for wages tied to the cost of living as a means of keeping wages down and thus of increasing the competitiveness of the Danish

Full employment was a central plank in Social Democrat election platforms in campaigns after 1945. This poster is unambiguous: "For full employment, vote Social Democrat". Photo: The Labour Movement's Library and Archive.

economy, but this course was flatly rejected by the trade union movement and thus also by the Social Democrats. The right-of-centre coalition was a minority government, and it had to accept compromise in order to survive. Commentators in *Jyllands-Posten* were totally opposed to any suggestion of increased control of industry. Instead, the aim should be for increased liberalisation of all aspects of the economy and a greater degree of geographical and occupational mobility, thus restricting the unions' "monopoly" of labour.

The constant sniping from the Social Democrats and the trade unions finally became so much of a problem, however, that in the September of 1952 the government announced that a number of public construction projects would be started during the winter. It was hoped that this initiative would help to avoid the persistently large fluctuations in seasonal unemployment figures. Nevertheless, *Social-Demokraten* continued to rail against the government's economic policy and its consequences for employment. With a general election known to be on its way as soon as the issue of a revision of the Constitution had been resolved in the spring of 1953, the paper took up its general Social Democratic themes ever more vociferously and clearly.

When the election campaign started in earnest in September 1953, *Vestkysten* and *Berlingske Tidende* in particular stressed that the right-of-centre parties could claim the credit for a full treasury and a balanced national budget. In addition, the combination of the seasonal summer upswing in employment and the improved international economic situation had brought unemployment down, allowing the newspapers to argue that "the employment situation has never been better", or words to that effect. Even when unemployment had been at its highest, it had not been above the level seen during the last period of the Social Democrat government, and the voices of the right were loud in proclaiming that unemployment had always been higher under Social Democrat governments than it had under governments of the right.

These views, however, found no echo in *Jyllands-Posten*, which was occupied with campaigning for the new right-of-centre party "The Independents". In the view of the paper this party would have a purer policy of the right and could thus bring the compromise-seeking outgoing coalition government back on course, should they be returned to power.

Unsurprisingly, *Social-Demokraten* persisted in highlighting unemployment as the key issue in the campaign, bringing it increasingly to the forefront. Since any realistic assessment of unemployment at that time had to be that it was not particularly severe, the paper chose to lead a scare campaign. Were its readers ready, the paper asked, to face future economic downturns under a government armed only with the credit squeeze, with consequent increased unemployment, as its weapon for overcoming financial crises?

For the Communist newspaper Land og Folk it scarcely mattered whether the election campaign of September 1953 produced a government of the right or by the Social Democrats; in either case, rearmament would continue and this would prevent a return to full employment. The party's election advertisement argued that there had been widespread unemployment under both the Social Democrat government of Hans Hedtoft and the right-of-centre coalition government that replaced the Social Democrats in 1950. Photo: The Danish Royal Library.

Politiken supported the Social Liberals' great idea of the formation of a broad centrist coalition after the election, to consist of the Social Liberals, the Liberals and the Social Democrats. As a result, it was not possible for the paper to use the theme of "the unemployed" too much in the election campaign, since this would inevitably lead to supporting the policy of one party or another from among the possible coalition group.

For the Communist paper *Land og Folk*, the arch-enemy was not necessarily the right-of-centre government. Instead, the targets of the paper's attacks were the Social Democrats and the Social Democratic trade unions who, it was claimed, were going directly against workers' interests through their backing of Denmark's "Atlantic Policy", i.e. membership of NATO. Rearmament led to unemployment, because its financing required increases in taxation. This taxation reduced the overall spending power in society, thus reducing demand and creating job losses.

4.2. The remainder of the 1950s: The "islands of unemployment"

The end result of the 1953 election was the formation of a minority Social Democrat government led by Hans Hedtoft. Despite the political colour of the government, unemployment continued to be widespread throughout the remainder of the 1950s, though it never returned to the levels of the 1920s and certainly not to those of the 1930s.

Unskilled workers bore the brunt of the unemployment, and in certain specific areas of Jutland the levels were extremely high, especially during winter months when little outdoor work was possible. The result was that the continuing newspaper debate on the unemployed during the 1950s focused to a high degree on the initiatives that the authorities could take with respect to the so-called "islands of unemployment" that had appeared, most especially in North and West Jutland.

The debate grew more intense when the Social Democrats took over the reins of government in October of 1953, with a very positive discussion of the situation appearing in *Social-Demokraten*. Behind the proposed solutions to a problem which was, when all was said and done, limited in extent lay certain Social Democrat visions of a more active industrial and labour market policy. At this early stage, the right-of-centre papers expressed no significant opposition to these ideas.

In April 1955 the Social Democrat government put forward a number of proposals that would see the state acting as the driving force behind the creation of long-term jobs, with the classical job-creation programmes of the public works type seen in 1930s receiving much lower priority. Examples of the new strategy included cheap loans to industry, loans to the fishing industry and loans for soil improvement. The government also made a declaration of its intent to locate new state offices in the areas affected by unemployment. In addition, there were various initiatives aimed at promoting mobility of labour. The government also stressed, to the approval of *Social-Demokraten*, that these strategies would be based exclusively on local initiatives, which would then receive state support.

Certain reservations began to appear in the comments of the right-of-centre press with respect to the elements of a planned economy which those on the orthodox right could detect in the proposals. Instead, the right-of-centre parties expressed their wish to see the emphasis on the initiatives regarding a significant increase in the geographical mobility of labour. The labour market in the area around Copenhagen had developed a high degree of mobility, and workers in certain trades had long since accepted that they had to take work wherever they could find it. Why could the same not be the case in the more remote regions of the country, and among the unskilled?

Nevertheless, the debate still remained at a rather muted level. The proposals for state support for soil improvement and the development of the fishing industry were very acceptable to the Liberal and Conservative parties, and the legislation passed through Parliament without any major problems – and according to the papers, without any strong political commitment either. It is clear, though, from the newspaper debate over the years that followed that the problems had not by any means been solved. The reforms were far from being sufficient, and the economic development that did take place had no impact on reducing unemployment in the affected areas.

In January 1957, with unemployment again at a relatively high level, the government set up yet another committee to look into the matter, and held meetings with local politicians in North Jutland. This prompted sharp criticism of the government in *Land og Folk* for having done nothing but set up a committee, and for failing to take any effective action in face of the unemployment situation. The problem was not simply a limited local one, according to the Communist paper, but reflected a wretched employment situation overall. There was little sympathy for the Communist view among the trade unions or the unemployed, but nevertheless a government with its power base among the working classes could scarcely ignore the problem of unemployment.

In the autumn of 1957 the debate was rekindled when a feature entitled "The neglected regions" by Viggo Kampmann, the Social Democrat Minister of Finance, was printed in *Dagens Nyheder*, which was the principal press voice of industrial interests. Through an analysis of the nature of the current unemployment situation in the Danish periphery – the chief characteristics of which were the numerous unskilled workers in the labour force, and a labour market for these workers which predominantly involved outdoor work and thus largely shut down during the winter – Kampmann reached the conclusion that the solution lay in locating small and medium-sized companies in North Jutland, the western part of South Jutland, West Jutland and perhaps parts of Lolland.

The state could contribute by developing the necessary infrastructure – and why stop there, asked the Minister? A concerned state could contribute to the financing of workshops and factories, and could also provide venture capital. Perhaps a system of state refunds would make it possible to reduce local taxes in these impoverished areas? To appease the trade unions, who wanted immediate results, the Minister added that it would be necessary during a transitional period to supplement these measures with more conventional public works projects, until the effects of the new policies made themselves felt.

By the end of the 1950s the general mood was turning towards the view that an actively interventionist state could be instrumental in promoting development generally and in resolving social problems. The "social engineers" of the welfare state – those who worked in the social services in various capacities – were making a growing impact, and perhaps beginning to make their presence felt more in the remoter regions of the country as well as in the capital. In any event, at the time of the opening of Parliament in October 1957, *Social-Demokraten* informed its readers that the government would take extraordinary initiatives to solve the problems of the "islands of unemployment".

Now a powerful voice from West Jutland made itself heard. Gunnar Andreasen, Managing Director of the chemical company Cheminova,[7] made a great impression in the Jutland press when he published a pamphlet entitled "The Future of West Jutland". The publication made the claim that the politicians and central administration did not care about the provinces. It went on to outline a plan for the industrial development of West Jutland, based on locally available raw materials (salt, fish, lignite and wood), on the proximity of the region to the industrial centre of Europe, and on the local labour force, which was dependable to a degree not found anywhere else in Denmark. *Jyllands-Posten* and *Vestkysten* backed this initiative strongly, referring at the same time to Viggo Kampmann's earlier article in *Dagens Nyheder*.

In the wake of the publication of Gunnar Andreasen's pamphlet, there were public meetings in West Jutland where the mood was one of enthusiasm and excitement, and these meetings were comprehensively covered by the Jutland press. According to the press reports, the Members of Parliament representing West Jutland backed the initiative unconditionally, and Andreasen very deliberately played on the contrast between the more responsive politicians and

---

[7] The factory had been forced to move from the Copenhagen area as a result of environmental regulations; see Jensen (1996).

the arrogant Copenhagen bureaucrats in the central administration. Other initiatives, such as the journey of a deputation of North Jutland trade unionists to Copenhagen for discussions with the government and Parliament in January 1958, also received widespread press coverage, in this instance in nearly all the papers included in this survey. The union representatives demanded a mix of traditional job-creating public works programmes, increased benefits, and initiatives to promote the establishment of private companies in the region.

According to an editorial in *Social-Demokraten* in January 1958, public opinion was in favour of the state stepping in to support local initiatives by creating better conditions for such enterprises to succeed, first and foremost by helping companies to overcome the financial barriers to local investment. On the other hand, the paper recognised that there was little public support for the idea of state-owned industry.

The government's next step, in the spring of 1958, was to introduce a parliamentary bill regarding regional development. The proposal included provisions regarding direct loans by the state or loan guarantees for new industry and support for project studies in connection with setting up new enterprises, all to be administered by a centralised state regional development council. The initiative was warmly welcomed by the government-supporting *Social-Demokraten* and *Politiken*, and *Social-Demokraten* could also point to support for the proposal from the trade unions.

However, when the bill was introduced in Parliament, the same papers had to report strong opposition from the right-of-centre parties during the first reading. The right-of-centre papers' explanation was that the Liberals feared that if the proposal became law, it would pave the way for the increased socialisation of industry and extend even further the bureaucratic machinery of the state. The Conservatives were also fiercely opposed to the bill, arguing that it would be better for the Government to reduce taxes and thus promote private saving and the associated opportunities for the financing of development. *Dagens Nyheder*, the voice of industry, propounded the same view, claiming in an editorial that the state was not able of itself to create prosperity – only to redistribute the problems of society.

The right-wing critics of the bill claimed that it was unclear in its scope. Soon the entire country to the west of the suburbs of Copenhagen would be demanding subsidies for industrial development! Economists also pointed out that the bill contained no criteria for determining the location of industries. Lacking all contact with reality, the law could easily be a complete fiasco, not least because of pressures from the establishment of new European markets where productivity would be the key in the light of increased competition.

After the passage of the Regional Development Act the newspaper debate continued over the implementation of the law, since the actual amounts of money available depended on annual negotiations in the Finance Committee. All the papers reported the right-wing opposition to ear-marking millions for subsidies during the budget negotiations in 1958. Early in the 1960s, however, the newspaper reports became less political in nature. Journalists reported on the outcomes of the law; the results were not found to be particularly impressive. Despite amendments to the act throughout the 1960s, the problem of the "islands of unemployment" had still not been resolved at the time of the last amendment to the law in 1972.

4.3. The long period of prosperity, 1959-73

In the national context, the problem of unemployment was resolved in around 1959-60 by a shortage of labour. This itself became a serious problem in the beginning of the 1960s, and in view of this and in particular in light of possible labour shortages in export industries a discussion arose concerning the import of guest-workers from overseas.

The debate intensified in the summer of 1964 as a result of a feature article in *Aktuelt* (*Social-Demokraten* changed name to Aktuelt in 1959) written by the then Minister of Trade, Hilmar Baunsgaard, who represented the Social Liberals in an otherwise Social Democrat government.

Without going into much detail, the article argued that the importation of foreign workers in a situation where there was a pressing shortage of labour could increase prosperity in the country, and this at a time when the general public were particularly interested in the ongoing increase in affluence. In the Minister's view, the alternative to the use of foreign labour was economic stagnation. Hilmar Baunsgaard's ideas on the use of foreign labour met with a storm of criticism from the papers, with the exception of *Jyllands-Posten* and *Politiken*. The opposition of the trade unions was most clearly expressed in *Aktuelt* – the paper that had started the debate in the first place – but was also reported in *Berlingske Tidende* and *Vestkysten*.

The representatives of the trade unions and the Social Democrat politicians took a line of argument that was to endure throughout the 1960s. Their view was that it was always preferable to invest in new technology – in part in order to maintain the country's competitiveness – rather than to import Southern European or Turkish labour, whose presence would contribute to depressing wages through competition for employment and would also tend to entrench old-fashioned production methods and systems. At the same time, it was pointed out that unemployment could easily return at any time, and also that there was in fact an unused reserve of labour in Denmark in the shape of married women. The most strongly opposed were the spokesmen for the unskilled, the group which had borne the brunt of unemployment in Denmark since industrialisation began. Several newspapers rejected the idea on the practical grounds that it would be impossible to attract foreign workers to the country. Another point raised during this first debate in the summer of 1964 was made in reports by several papers on the situation in Germany and Switzerland on the effects of the presence of large numbers of foreign workers. These reports were by no means unequivocally positive.

The years of prosperity and the associated massive development of the welfare state, with the Social Democrats at the helm of government and the Social Liberals as their steadfast coalition allies, saw the revision of the almost sixty-year-old law on unemployment funds which, with its later offshoots, had led to the introduction of a series of means-tested benefits administered by the funds.

The Social Democrat Minister of Labour, Erling Dinesen, set up a committee in 1964 to study the question of the revision. In 1966 this committee produced an interim report, which received detailed coverage in all the papers included in this survey. The interim report recommended considerably increased levels of benefit. This was completely in tune with the mood of the times; it was felt that the state had an obligation to compensate for loss of income arising as a result of social conditions, in accordance with the "principle of solidarity".

This principle of solidarity meant that members of all unemployment funds that received the same levels of benefit should also pay the same level of subscription, regardless of the degree of unemployment in the professional area covered by that fund, and the state should assume the additional risk involved in the event of changes in levels of unemployment. These ideas have to be viewed against a background of an unemployment level of around 2% of the labour force.

The newspaper debate surrounding the parliamentary bill which the Minister of Labour introduced testifies to surprisingly widespread support for the idea of rises in the level of benefits. Equally surprising was the political message from the right, as quoted in, for example, *Berlingske Tidende*, proclaiming the need for a speedy increase in unemployment benefits – a pronouncement which caused *Politiken* to accuse conservative politicians of starting the next election campaign prematurely.

In any event, the political messages in the newspapers of the time were marked by a surprising unanimity of view on the issue of unemployment legislation. The earlier arguments that payments at too high a level could destroy the will to work rather than collect unemployment benefit had now largely vanished. The fact that the state would assume the whole of the financial risk that was involved, which could lead to budgetary problems in the event of any future steep rise in unemployment, was only alluded to indirectly in a single Social Liberal commentary.

The unanimity did not extend to views on wage increases. The right-of-centre papers warned against any rapid rise in wages. They predicted that wage increases would lead to inflation and thus, in the long term, could harm the prospects for continued full employment. They were supported by the Danish Economic Council, which had argued since its foundation in 1962 in favour of an incomes policy.

Such views were rejected by *Aktuelt*, however. According to the Danish Confederation of Trade Unions, wages were simply mirroring productivity, which was also clearly at a high level. Any wage increase below the level of growth in productivity would contribute to increasing economic inequalities in society. If unemployment did occur, then this was due to the international economic cycle, on which a small country like Denmark could have no influence.

The international economy fared badly in 1967, and Danish unemployment rose in the autumn of that year. The Social Democrat government was defeated in Parliament in December of 1967 over the issue of freezing cost of living allowances in an attempt to restrict inflation. The Social Democrats and *Aktuelt* identified unemployment as the principal issue in the subsequent election, and the right-of-centre parties and papers followed suit.

The Social Democrats, through the pages of *Aktuelt*, claimed just as in the 1950s that a right-wing government would conduct an economic policy which would further increase the level of unemployment that had been created by the international economic crisis. The right-of-centre papers, on the other hand, pointed to the fact that unemployment had risen under a Social Democratic government and a socialist majority in Parliament. This government's mismanagement had contributed to the economic mess, they said, and the socialist majority in Parliament had caused anxiety in the top echelons of business – the implication being that this had created a bad climate for investment. A right-of-centre government, in contrast, would pursue business-friendly policies which would lead to a return to full employment.

The debate in January 1968 demonstrated that despite 6-7 years of near full employment, the fear of unemployment was still present in the population. The impression of the 1960s as a carefree period was not altogether accurate. For the unskilled, especially those living in the outer regions of the country, unemployment remained a part of everyday life that they had to cope with from time to time – even during the economic boom of the 1960s.

Developments from 1968 until 1973 can be summarised briefly as follows. The pressure from the trade union movement and the political left for a coherent Danish guest worker policy that built up at the end of the 1960s reached its peak in the autumn of 1970. The result was a temporary halt to the issue of new work permits for foreigners. It is also apparent from the debate in the newspapers and in Parliament that a majority of the population desired stricter controls in this area, and that in addition many politicians felt there should be a pause in the granting of work permits while Parliament formulated a clear policy. Any disagreement among the papers and the politicians concerned the length of the temporary halt. The right-of-centre papers wanted a flexible period of suspension, so that any pressing shortage of labour in a particular sector of the economy could be solved by allowing in more workers, while the trade unions and the left-of-centre press were in favour of a more comprehensive cessation of the import of foreign labour.

A constantly recurring argument against guest workers in the second half of the 1960s and onward was the fear that they would push Danish workers into unemployment. The article above concerns a group of Turks being attacked by a gang of bikers. The justification for this attack was that "The Turks are taking our jobs" (Aktuelt, 13 May 1969). Photo: The Danish Royal Library.

4.4. The oil crisis, autumn 1973

When the oil crisis struck in the autumn of 1973, with accompanying prophecies in the media of gloom, doom and rising unemployment as a result of supply problems, views on the use of guest workers become more convergent.

The majority of politicians, and thus also of the newspapers, agreed – at least for a while – on the need to exclude new foreign workers completely, even though *Berlingske Tidende* hinted strongly that these workers were being made a scapegoat in a situation over which the Danish government actually had little control. For their part, the trade unions felt that the fears that had been expressed in the 1960s had proved fully justified: in a time of recession, Danish workers were being fired before foreigners.

The character of the debate altered once more during the 1970s as the pattern of immigration shifted from being a matter of movement of labour to one of family reunification, and thus of increasing demands on the welfare state; it was at this time that the theme of "unemployed foreign workers" started to come into the picture. A contributing factor was that the political vacuum caused by the lack of any home for opinions critical of foreigners, as identified by a reader of *Vestkysten* in 1970, was filled with the establishment of the populist, anti-taxation, anti-bureaucratic Progress Party and that party's triumphant entry into Parliament in the election of 1973. Some conservative politicians began to express views that were more critical of guest workers than had been the case before the economic downturn; such views seem to have been particularly frequently articulated in *Jyllands-Posten*. On the left, however, such criticisms were described as constituting a witch-hunt against foreigners.

In the spring of 1974 the newspapers reflected the political disagreement over how seriously the oil crisis and the general economic situation would affect employment. As early as January 1974, *Aktuelt* was warning of serious impending levels of unemployment, and the paper accused the Liberal government under its Prime Minister, Poul Hartling, of wanting to solve the problems of hyperinflation and catastrophic trade figures by means of economic policies that he ought to know would be certain to increase unemployment. In contrast, *Berlingske Tidende* continued to deny that any problem of massive unemployment was in the offing. On the contrary, argued the paper, business was still suffering from major shortages of labour. *Jyllands-Posten*, *Politiken* and *Vestkysten* all expressed opinions on similar lines, though the picture shifted a little at times. All the papers reported the unequivocal view of the government's economic think-tank that an incomes policy was necessary to solve the country's deep-rooted economic problems and thus to ensure continued employment.

Early on, opinion polls showed a majority to be against the importation of guest workers. On 26 October 1970, for example, Berlingske Tidende published an article presenting the results of a survey of public opinions on foreign workers. The headline read "No to the Importation of Guest Workers". Photo: The Danish Royal Library.

By the summer of 1974 the signs of an economic crisis were becoming clearer, and in August of that year the majority of the papers reported the broad political agreement that employment levels were seriously threatened. *Aktuelt* criticised the government's economic policy in the most severe terms, and spokesmen for the Social Democrats and the Confederation of Trade Unions demanded through the paper that the government should take measures to stimulate employment. But, in the view of *Aktuelt*, it remained the most cynical intention of the government to use unemployment as part of its economic strategy, by allowing unemployment to restrict wage rises and thus improve the balance of payments and the competitiveness of Danish companies. Like *Aktuelt*, *Politiken* used its editorial columns to criticise the government for an indefensible economic policy that allowed unemployment to grow without intervening, but when the former Social Democrat Prime Minister, Anker Jørgensen, put forward a proposal that employees should be given a veto over the winding up of companies, the paper backed off. The reasons for this were not entirely clear, but probably Anker Jørgensen's proposal smacked too much of state control of production in the eyes of the Social Liberal paper.

Berlingske Tidende, *Jyllands-Posten* and *Vestkysten* argued for the introduction of an incomes policy and for transferring labour from the construction sector to export industries. The press reports show that the government discussed incomes policy solutions with the parties to the labour market, and that the Confederation of Trade Unions indicated that under certain conditions – including the maintenance of real wage levels and a move towards profit sharing schemes – they might be able to accept an incomes policy solution.

When the government put forward an employment plan at the end of August 1974, it was met with overwhelmingly negative press comment, except in the pages of *Vestkysten*. According to that paper, the claim by leading Social Democrats and trade unionists that the government was responsible for the rising level of unemployment was pure political manipulation; the real causes were the worsening international economic situation, high wages and an unfavourable balance of trade. In addition, the government had already removed a ban on municipal building projects and other public works schemes.

In the early autumn of 1974, *Aktuelt* ran a particularly forthright campaign on the theme of unemployment. The building industry had been especially severely hit, with an unemployment level of around 7% during the sector's busiest period of the year. The paper gave Anker Jørgensen free rein to present a continued critique of the Liberal government's economic policies, which it was claimed created unemployment. The accusation that the government was deliberately using unemployment to stop inflation and remove the trade deficit again appeared in both the news coverage and the editorial comment. One editorial claimed that the government wanted to create a new type of social equality on a much lower economic level, with high unemployment and general underutilisation of production capacity. In a somewhat ambivalent manner, *Aktuelt* also reported on the Copenhagen building workers' Communist-led actions.

During the summer and autumn of 1974, *Aktuelt* reported the new opinions being voiced by trade unionists concerning the movement's possible acceptance of an incomes policy as part of a solution to the nation's economic imbalances. However, in September 1974 the Executive Committee of the Confederation of Trade Unions demanded as a precondition for the movement's acceptance of an incomes policy that the government should not operate economic policies that would create further unemployment. Furthermore, the demand that profit-sharing should be included in any agreement was ever present.

While *Aktuelt* published a large number of articles on the unemployment issue during September 1974, the right-of-centre papers gave it less prominent coverage. *Berlingske Tidende*, for example, published considerably fewer articles, but the paper also adopted a very concerned tone. It rejected classical Keynesian policies as a strategy for solving the economic crisis. To be sure, unemployment could be reduced through economic and monetary policy, but Denmark already had a large foreign debt as a result of the borrowing in the 1960s, and now there were many other countries seeking loans on the international money markets. *Berlingske Tidende* quoted unnamed economists as saying that in the prevailing situation it would be foolish to attempt economic interventions that would keep unemployment artificially low. That would just postpone a real resolution of the problem, while making the economic situation even worse. Instead it was necessary to implement a tight incomes policy. Referring to analyses recently published by the Danish Economic Council's executive, the paper argued that salaries should be reduced and cost-of-living allowances suspended. On the other hand, *Berlingske Tidende* did not recommend devaluation as the way forward.

Politiken's discussion of the unemployment problem in September 1974 revealed that European conservative politicians had aired the idea that unemployment of a certain level might be necessary in order to solve the problems of high inflation. In the light of this, *Politiken* had to insist once more on its view that an incomes policy was the right solution. *Jyllands-Posten* similarly argued for an incomes policy and for a better targeted policy for helping Danish industry, while *Vestkysten* continued to defend the existing government strategy.

After the opening of Parliament, *Aktuelt* intensified its campaign for the government to call an election, so that there could be a new *Folketing* with the capacity to fight unemployment more effectively.

4.5. In the grip of the crisis, 1976-82

By 1976 no-one in Denmark could be in any doubt that unemployment was here to stay, and more opinion polls commissioned by the newspapers concerned this topic than any other during that year. Editorials and other commentaries in the papers made direct links between the results of these surveys and the ways politicians could attempt to solve the problem.

The most direct link was made in *Børsen*, a financial daily, which found evidence in one such opinion poll conducted for the paper that the general public were willing to exercise wage restraint within the framework of an incomes policy. There was even a majority of those surveyed who were prepared to accept a 10% reduction in salary if this would have a positive effect on employment. The paper challenged the politicians to take into account the people's willingness to make sacrifices and, on this basis, to introduce a carefully targeted incomes policy. Interviews with leading unionists, also published in *Børsen*, indicated that the trade union movement was gradually becoming more open to the idea of a keeping wage increases at a very modest level. The unions did, however, want to maintain the level of wages in real terms. One point that emerged from the analyses of the opinion surveys was that many people believed that the level of unemployment benefit was too high: so high, in fact, that it reduced the will to seek new employment.

Towards the end of the 1970s the right-of-centre papers kept returning to the topic of "the abuse of benefit payments"; this would have been unthinkable during the building up of the welfare state in the 1960s. The Confederation of Danish Employers argued in the pages of *Berlingske Tidende* for a readjustment of benefit payments, since the high levels of benefit current at that time obliged companies to raise wages beyond the point that could be justified by their output simply in order to attract sufficient employees. Other articles pointed out that long-term unemployment made the unemployed almost unemployable, because they had discovered a new way of life with greater freedom to enjoy the many opportunities afforded by a modern society: in other words, they acquired a taste for a life of leisure financed by the state.

In contrast, towards the end of the 1970s *Aktuelt* was arguing in the face of the prospect of increasing unemployment as a result of the second oil crisis that the state should extend its schemes related to the unemployed with plans for job creation and investment, offers of work for the long-term unemployed, and early retirement schemes. The long-term unemployed who were members of unemployment funds and who were available for work should be offered nine months of work, the amount they needed to reacquire the right to benefits. The government stressed that the scheme should ensure that the unemployed maintained their ability to work, or in the words of Svend Auken, the Minister for Labour, that the working abilities of the unemployed should be maintained through retraining in skills needed by society.

When the government introduced a bill to this effect it gained a relatively warm reception from the centrist parties in Parliament, and the newspaper debate was marked by general unanimity that the bill was necessary. There was however some scepticism among the parties of the right concerning the financing of the scheme, and with respect to what would happen when the period of employment was over. Would the people who had participated in job creation schemes once more find themselves unemployed?

At a time when the Social Democrats' monopoly on power had still not been seriously threatened, *Aktuelt* did not hesitate to make barely concealed threats against the business community: if the private sector would not make the necessary investment to secure employment, the state would have to step in. As it had done in the 1930s, the paper also demanded a ban on overtime – a demand echoed by the Social Democrat Minister of Labour. From time to time the notion of an incomes policy was also aired in the Social Democratic newspaper, but it was clear that the policy should take a restrained and "socially responsible" form, i.e. that it should not threaten any reduction in real wages.

In the autumn of 1978, a new Social Democrat and Liberal coalition government under the premiership of Anker Jørgensen passed a bill on an early retirement scheme, to the approval of *Aktuelt* and *Politiken* and with largely neutral comment in *Vestkysten*. The scheme allowed members of unemployment funds who were aged 60-66 to withdraw from the labour market on benefits equivalent to full unemployment pay, though the amount was gradually reduced after 2½ years. The far left had reservations about the scheme, criticising it for not being sufficiently generous to people in the age range of 60-66; and early on in the negotiations over the proposal the Social Liberals attempted to use the early retirement scheme as a stalking horse for a general revision of the unemployment insurance system which would remove it entirely from the unemployment funds and transfer its administration to the state.

Together with the Conservative Party, *Berlingske Tidende* criticised the early retirement scheme as potential being very expensive for the state and for society in general. It would lead to greater demands on state finances, and it would encourage civil servants, feeling that the value of their own pension schemes was being reduced relative to those of other employees, to increase their demands in the approaching salary negotiations. The right-wing Progress Party, with its founder and leader Mogens Glistrup to the fore, criticised the proposal as being yet another offshoot of a state system that was growing out of control. *Jyllands-Posten* emphasised the widespread lack of agreement in Parliament concerning the early retirement scheme, in particular with respect to the extent it could be expected to result in older employees being forced to leave the labour market.

At an early stage in the negotiation process, in the spring of 1978, the Liberals and the Social Liberals made the criticism that the scheme was too exclusive, in that the self-employed would find difficulty in meeting the requirements for early retirement. However, this problem was remedied through some adjustments to the bill, which was reintroduced in October 1978. Because of this, and because the Liberal Party had now entered government as a coalition partner with the Social Democrats, the objections were withdrawn, and the two parties both voted in favour of the bill. The new law came into force on 1 January 1979.

One notable feature of all the contributions to the debate on the early retirement scheme in the course of 1978 was that they consistently underestimated the built-in potential of the scheme to act as an incentive to withdraw early from the labour market. In the years that followed, many more people opted to take early retirement than had been predicted in the ministerial calculations made to assess the likely consequences of the proposal. The Social Liberals, for example, stressed in 1978 – before they knew the extent of the uptake – that the early retirement scheme should be maintained as a welfare benefit for the elderly even if there was a return to full employment.

While all the main parties, including the Conservatives, debated the entitlement and possible exclusion of particular (voter) groups, the only party to object against the whole principle of the scheme was the Progress Party. The party believed that the new addition to the state bureaucratic machinery – to be financed in part by employers – would be of no help in getting the young (and the youngish) into employment. The early retirement scheme would thus, the party argued, increase the demands on an already hard-pressed business sector and as a result actually push more people out of work.

One sole article by an American researcher and expert in age-related issues, published in *Berlingske Tidende*, made the point that schemes which obliged or encouraged the elderly to leave the labour market "before time" constituted an attack on certain inalienable Western rights, such as the right of the elderly to seek happiness unhindered by regulations imposed by society. Another lone article – published in *Aktuelt*, perhaps surprisingly – claimed that schemes that excluded older workers from the labour force would reduce the flexibility of the labour market, and thus create new unemployment.

Both unemployment and large budgetary imbalances persisted; the Social Democrats, as the ruling party, were proving incapable of coming up with effective strategies to combat these major problems. The Social Democrats were also under pressure from the Confederation of Trade Unions, a factor which restricted their freedom to manoeuvre.

In September 1982 the Social Democrat government surrendered power to a centre-right coalition, consisting of the Liberals, the Conservatives and two small centre parties. At that time, unemployment was running at a level of about 12-13% of those who were members of unemployment insurance funds. Neither the Social Democratic Party nor the trade union movement had been able to devise convincing strategies to combat the combined problems of unemployment, inflation, the balance of payments deficit and the deficit in public finances. Splits within the party, within the trade union movement and between the party and the unions were more evident than ever before in the coverage by all the newspapers in this survey. It was difficult, if not impossible, to unite the various splinter groups to make a concerted effort against unemployment and the balance of payments deficit.

The centre-right parties and their affiliated newspapers felt that their day had come at last: it was time for a paradigm shift in Danish politics.

4.6. The debate on unemployment under a centre-right government, 1982-84

In the autumn of 1982, *Aktuelt* reported the rejection by the Social Democrats and the trade union movement of the proposal by the new centre-right government to reduce public spending and to intervene in wage formation. The party and the unions may indeed have accepted that there was a need for some adjustment, but not surprisingly attacked the government for wanting to introduce a policy that would have detrimental social consequences. Their comments reflected classic Social Democrat themes. The costs of balancing the budget and reducing the balance of payments deficit would fall primarily on wage earners and more especially on the unemployed and others on the margins of society. *Aktuelt* hammered home the same message time after time during the autumn of 1982. Immediately after the new government took office, the tone was less confrontational, but when the government's politico-economic proposal was put forward in October 1982 the criticisms became shrill and insistent. *Aktuelt* also devoted intensive coverage to the responses to the government policy: there were major demonstrations, strikes and other protests during the autumn of 1982, all fully reported by the paper. At the same time, the paper emphasised that the proposal would create more unemployment, while any effects on the balance of payments and the public budget deficit would take a long time to make themselves felt.

In September 1982 *Politiken* urged political moderation by inviting unity across the centre ground in combating the nation's economic woes, including measures to tackle the continuing high level of unemployment, primarily through the application of an incomes policy. When the new centre-right government was formed, predicted the newspaper, it would at first be paralysed and unable to act. After the installation of the new government, however, *Politiken* announced its suspicion that major changes in economic policy were on the way, and it warned against the dissolution of the welfare state, which would hit the unemployed particularly hard. When the compromise settlement was in place, the paper distanced itself strongly from its social consequences; as an old social liberal publication, *Politiken* found it disgraceful that the Social Liberals had been collaborators in passing through Parliament what the newspaper called "the black package". In the period that followed, *Politiken* added its voice to those making dire predictions of yet further increases in the already record high levels of unemployment.

Berlingske Tidende was unreservedly delighted that the parties of the centre and the right had succeeded in forming a government. Various articles argued that the business climate had to be improved in order to create more jobs. Other articles inveighed against the unemployment insurance system, leaving readers of the paper with the impression that the system invited abuse, and that the levels and duration of benefit were ridiculously generous. This prevented the labour market from functioning optimally, since wage increases were not geared to changes in productivity. The tone of the debate was noticeably harsher in the autumn of 1982 than it had been in the 1960s, for example during the debate over the very extensive reform of the unemployment insurance system in 1966-67. Opinion polls indicated a clear awareness of the crisis among the general public, expressed for example in the widespread understanding of the necessity for cuts in public spending.

Jyllands-Posten emphasised the seriousness of the country's economic problems, which it said were the worst since 1945. The Social Democrats had clung to power without having the ability to develop and implement the kind of policies needed to meet the challenge of the international economic crisis. It would be dangerous now if the trade unions and the Social Democrats were to decide to be obstructive. The government's aims should be to reduce the level of unemployment, the balance of payments deficit and the budget deficit. *Jyllands-Posten* stressed the pragmatism of the conservative Prime Minister, Poul Schlüter, and the fact that the government was so clearly prioritising the tackling of the nation's economic problems before all else; the paper only feared that Poul Schlüter might end up putting Social Democratic policies into practice.

When the new government's extensive legislative initiatives were in the final stages of negotiations in Parliament, in fact on 16 October 1982, the very day when agreement was reached, *Jyllands-Posten*'s front-page headline read "Absolute majority among voters in favour of the crisis legislation". An "Observa" survey conducted for the paper showed that in the light of the country's dire economic situation, an absolute majority of voters agreed with *all* the government's proposals.

After Poul Schlüter's opening speech to Parliament on 5 October 1982, *Berlingske Tidende* not only gave its unequivocal support to the government's economic policies, but went so far as to dismiss outright an objection from the Danish Confederation of Employers to the government's intervention in existing labour market agreements. The paper presented a whole series of conservative arguments focusing on the view that Denmark was on course for an economic catastrophe. Furthermore, the paper reported the view that the abuse of state benefits, including unemployment pay, was widespread, and that this was what was really threatening the welfare state to a much greater extent than prudent financial adjustments to the system. Nor did the paper neglect to report the opinion polls that documented widespread public support for drastic economic remedies. The question of whether these measures would increase unemployment was insignificant in the context of the necessity for a general economic shake-up. Unless the health of the economy was restored, there would be no welfare state in ten years' time, argued *Berlingske Tidende*.

Aktuelt made a notable contribution to the mobilisation of the trade union movement against the new centre-right government. That mobilisation in turn made a major contribution to some huge demonstrations outside the Parliament building during the debate on the bill. The rhetoric from the paper was not by any means a denial of the need for a degree of reorganisation in the economy – that was widely accepted within the Social Democratic movement – but an expression of the view of the party and the trade union movement that the reforms were too radical, and involved creating a degree of social imbalance that had not been seen in Denmark since the 1920s. Once the bill had been passed, *Aktuelt* gave an estimate that a further 60,000 workers would be thrown out of work as a consequence of the new government's economic policy.

Politiken took a similarly rejectionist line, based on similar arguments. *Politiken*'s views on the matter were so strong, in fact, that this one-time shaper of Social Liberal opinion now denounced the party for its complicity in the proposal.

When the government presented its "investment package" in December 1982, with incentives for increased investment in housing and business, the papers divided as before. *Aktuelt* and *Politiken* were strongly opposed to this piece of legislation, their arguments including the point that one of the components of the scheme to privatise elements of the public sector would lead to increased unemployment. *Berlingske Tidende*, *Jyllands-Posten* and *Vestkysten* could all see good elements in the plan, which they said would improve the Danish business climate and encourage technological advances. If the current shake-up of the economy could be followed by a successful outcome in the collective wage bargaining round with only moderate wage increases, then the future would look a lot brighter, they said.

With economic conditions improving and the government managing to hold the four parties in the coalition together, the Social Democrats and the trade unions began to realise that the centre-right group of parties might maintain their hold on power for a long time to come. In August of 1983, therefore, in an attempt to strengthen their party's credibility as a viable alternative government, the Social Democrats and the trade unions put forward their "S-plan". The workers' movement wished to discuss five important points with the government, namely social reconstruction, tax reform, a just incomes policy, increased investment and a reduction in the working week.

In the months that followed, opposition to the government became more intense; the Social Democrats aimed at bringing down the government, and in December 1983 the balance of votes in Parliament led to the calling of an election for January 1984.

During the election campaign, *Berlingske Tidende*, *Jyllands-Posten* and *Vestkysten* all stressed that the centre-right government was making good progress with its work on reforming the economy. Poul Schlüter was quoted as saying that the Danish economy of the 1980s was in better shape than that of the 1960s, even if unemployment was still high – for was that level of unemployment not on its way down?

There was much to indicate that this was indeed the case, to judge from various articles in the three papers, and according to *Berlingske Tidende* this rather hampered the Social Democrat election campaign, which centred on the unemployed and the fear of unemployment felt by those in work. The demand made by the unions and the Social Democrats that the working week should be shortened in Denmark in face of the prevailing unemployment situation, without there being any corresponding adjustment in other European countries, was rejected by the three papers as unrealistic, since such a move would reduce Danish competitiveness and thus create further unemployment. If the government could only hold its course, said *Berlingske Tidende*, *Jyllands-Posten* and *Vestkysten*, then there was every prospect that 1984 would be "a year of economic celebration", just as 1983 had been a very good year with strong rises on the stock market, falling inflation, and a declining deficit in both the balance of payments and the national budget. In an interview shortly before the election, Poul Schlüter predicted that the Danish economy would finally be fully reorganised if the four-party coalition were returned for another four years in power.

Politiken found it difficult to support the Social Liberals in the election campaign, given their acceptance of the government's economic policies. The newspaper expressed its doubts about the economic results claimed by the centre-right coalition government, and urged that instead there should be a coalition between the Social Democrats, the Socialist People's Party and the Social Liberals. However, the Social Liberals let it be known that they would not support a Social Democrat government.

In the view of *Aktuelt* – a view seconded by leading spokesmen for the unions – inequality and class conflict had increased during the short time the four-party coalition had been in power. The government was also accused of having damaged the "Danish Model" of the labour market by not involving both sides in discussions over changes in the way the market operated.

Aktuelt published a plan by the Social Democrats and the unions for an alternative policy that would put 200,000 more people into work by 1990. This plan included a reduction in the length of the working week as a realistic possibility. If Denmark remained a "Schlüter society" until 1990, however, unemployment would stay at around the 300,000 level, the paper claimed. The Confederation of Trade Unions declared the coming contest to be "the unions' election". At the same time, *Aktuelt* stressed that the Social Democrats would be an economically responsible party of government, and that the fact was that only the Social Democrats, with their close contact with the unions, could implement an incomes policy that was both stringent *and* just.

At election meetings, the main theme was the classic debate on unemployment: "Who is responsible for the level of unemployment?" "Who has worked to reduce it?" That was the basic tenor of the debate on the correct interpretation of changes in the levels of unemployment under Poul Schlüter.

The Social Democrat campaign missed its mark, and the centre-right government was re-elected until the resignation of Poul Schlüter in 1993.

4.7. After 1993: the debate under a Social Democrat-led government

After the change in government in 1993, all the newspapers warned of the worsening economic climate and the poor immediate outlook for the Danish economy. Nevertheless, the new government under the leadership of Poul Nyrup Rasmussen (Social Democrat) insisted that it would succeed in combating unemployment, though it would be a question of a long haul, and that it would be necessary to make a new start from scratch. *Aktuelt*, and to a lesser extent *Politiken*, backed this view of the situation, and the new government – consisting of the Social-Democrats, the Social Liberals and two small centre parties – received good press in these two papers, both of which insisted on the necessity for an active labour market policy. *Politiken* quoted Marianne Jelved, the Social Liberal Finance Minister, as saying that unemployment could only be brought down if wage increases continued to be low – thus positioning herself within a classical Social Liberal tradition that in favour of income policy could be traced back to the incomes policy debates of the 1960s.

Among the right-of-centre papers, *Jyllands-Posten* and *JydskeVestkysten* were the most critical of the new government. *Jyllands-Posten* demanded a comprehensive reform of the social system, while *JydskeVestkysten* attacked the government for having a vision for a labour market that would be no better than the bankrupt systems of Eastern Europe. All talk of a "third labour market" based on more or less artificial job creation schemes in the public sector would in practice only lead to reduced efficiency in the labour market and society. The two papers reported public scepticism as to whether the shift in political power in Parliament would make any real difference, given the very difficult economic situation prevailing when the government assumed power.

After the passing of the government's labour market reform laws in June 1993, *Aktuelt* was at pains to emphasise that this was a clear indication of the power of the government to act and of the commitment to reducing unemployment. The reform was presented as having the specific goal of strengthening the activation element of the unemployment benefit legislation, while at the same time reducing the passive element of collecting benefit. The paper noted that another benefit of the reform was that it not only placed emphasis on the retraining of the unemployed in order to avoid problems of labour shortages in particular fields, but that it also gave due weight to the opportunities for individuals to choose their field of employment, and to the rights of the unemployed. Finally, the paper drew attention to the way in which the scheme for occupational leave introduced by the reform would create opportunities for job rotation, to the benefit of those out of work.

Politiken, too, commented that the reform was a necessary move, that it would create incentives for people to participate in education and training, and that the occupational leave scheme would stimulate job rotation. However, in an interview with Marianne Jelved, the Finance Minister, the paper also drew attention to the fact that there would now be a limit on the length of time for which claimants could draw unemployment benefit, even though no reductions had been made in the actual amount of the allowance. The way forward, said the paper, lay in further emphasis on training, and on changing the financing of unemployment benefit so that wage earners became more directly responsible for covering the costs involved.

Berlingske Tidende and *Jyllands-Posten* were essentially neutral in their comment on the labour market reform, while the most critical commentary could once again be found in *JydskeVestkysten*.

In August 1994 the Prime Minister, Poul Nyrup Rasmussen, called a snap election, to be held on 21 September. With a continued high level of unemployment and the basis on which the government had been founded – "A new start" – still fresh in the public memory, the foremost topic in the election campaign was the unemployed and the combating of unemployment.

Aktuelt, in addition to raising the spectre of a Conservative-Liberal-Progress Party alliance coming to power, emphasised that the Social Democrats had no wish to introduce more stringent rules concerning the requirement that the unemployed be available for work, or indeed any other tightening of the unemployment benefit regulations. The right-wing alliance, according to *Aktuelt*, would slash benefits and shorten the length of the period of entitlement. The paper also argued that the level of unemployment was falling – a claim that was immediately torpedoed by the publication by Statistics Denmark on 9 September of the unemployment figures for July, which showed that unemployment was once again on the increase. During the last phases of the election campaign, *Aktuelt* devoted much column space to refuting these statistics. In fact, the paper made its own survey of unemployment funds, which apparently showed that on the contrary, unemployment was declining rapidly.

Politiken similarly attempted to terrify the voters with the prospect of an unholy alliance of the right. This right-wing block would implement a crude, socially unjust reform of the unemployment benefit rules, a change that would ensure that those who were weakest in relation to the labour market would also be the worst off with respect to the benefits system. The messages from the Conservative and Liberal camps were, however, rather ambiguous, according to *Politiken*, in that talk from the Liberals during the election campaign suggested that they were weakening in their demand for a tightening up of the benefit rules.

While *Politiken* and *Aktuelt* devoted much space in their columns to warning their readers against an alliance of the Liberals, Conservatives and Progress Party, *Berlingske Tidende* worked hard to point out the threat to the nations economy posed by the Socialist People's Party, should it ever gain influence as a part of a Social Democrat-led government. The party favoured strengthening the rights of the unemployed, but had not thought through the economic consequences this would have, the paper claimed.

Towards the end of the election campaign in particular, *Berlingske Tidende* also reported the arguments of the right of that the current economically irresponsible government had singularly failed to break the rising trend in unemployment, with the occupational leave regulations having had nothing but a cosmetic effect on the jobless total. This economic irresponsibility had created a huge deficit in the state finances, and the consequent rises in interest rates were likely to halt or reverse the current upswing in the economy. The worst possible scenario would be a government made up of a coalition of the Social Democrats, the Socialists People's Party and the far-left "Unity List". The labour market regulations they would introduce would not bring unemployment down significantly before the associated wage increases weakened Danish competitiveness and put more people out of work.

However, *Berlingske Tidende* also reported the arguments of the Social Democrats and the Social Liberals concerning the socially irresponsible opposition who wanted to slash the level of unemployment benefit in order to pave the way for a lower minimum wage. This might get more people into work, the argument ran, but it would increase inequality and poverty in Denmark.

The election saw a new Social-Democrat-led government returned to power, and for the remainder of the decade the regime enjoyed the benefits of an improving economic situation and falling levels of unemployment.

4.8. Conclusion

If we consider the general picture presented by this analysis, it is clear that no single paper reported all aspects of the debate on the unemployed over the entire period of the survey. Anyone with a broad political interest would at any given time have had to read a selection of papers to get a complete overview of all opinions.

Over the course of the period, however, an increasing gap emerged between on the one hand the comment sections of the papers, in particular the editorials, which followed the political traditions of the different publications and their typical stances on the unemployed, and on the other hand the political reporting and general news coverage of the subject; thus we see that readers of all the different papers became increasingly well informed regarding opinions across the political spectrum. In this respect, the reporting of the debate on the unemployed is no different from the general trend seen in the development of Danish newspapers over the period, as described by, for example, the newspaper historian Jette Drachmann Søllinge. Since the turn of the millennium, the focus of the debate has largely shifted to the issue of labour shortages and the question of importation of foreign labour.

References

Jensen, Bent. 1996. *Træk af miljødebatten i seks danske aviser fra 1870'erne til 1970'erne*. Copenhagen: Statistics Denmark.

Appendix 1

A quantitative analysis of the debate in *Berlingske Tidende* and *Social-Demokraten/Aktuelt* 1900-1990

This book has outlined the newspaper debate on the unemployed in the most important Danish newspapers from the end of absolutism in 1848 until the turn of the millennium. Obviously, neither all the articles printed, nor all the issues raised, have been discussed – there simply would not have been enough space for this in the book – but the most important and representative themes and debates have been covered. A more fully documented discussion of the debate is to be found in the three separate volumes that the Rockwool Foundation Research Unit published in 2006 and 2008.[8]

This Appendix discusses another important aspect of the theme, namely the *intensity* of the debate at any given time, through a systematic count of the number of articles published in two of the papers in the period 1900-1990. It thus provides a supplement to the qualitative analysis, and highlights certain structural trends evident over the course of the 20th century. As with the qualitative analysis, the concept of "the unemployed" has been used as the main search term; see also Chapter 1, where the use of the ILO definition is discussed. "Debate" is again defined in the broadest possible sense as anything which is aimed at influencing opinion. In addition to the core meaning of the word, then, as a more or less direct dialogue between two or more debaters, it is to be regarded here as encompassing newspaper editorials, background feature articles, reports of proceedings in both chambers of Parliament (after 1953 only the Folketing), reports of political or occupational group meetings, cartoons, and advertisements of activities related to the unemployed.

The data used

The quantitative analysis is based on texts published in two politically opposed newspapers, *Berlingske Tidende* and *Social-Demokraten/Aktuelt*, during the period 1900 to 1990. For reasons of the sheer quantity of work that would have been involved, it has not been possible within the framework of this project to read through both newspapers for each day of the whole 90-year period. Instead, the analysis is based on a sample drawn by a reading of the two papers for the months of January and September of each year in the period studied.

In earlier times in particular, unemployment has seen strong seasonal variation in many trades, as has been noted in this book. Unskilled outdoor labourers in general, and workers in the building industry in particular, were especially badly

---

[8] Jensen (2006, 2007 and 2008).

hit by seasonal variations, since outdoor construction work often had to stop during the winter months; but other industries have also experienced low points during the winter, especially during the early years of this survey. It is in order to capture these seasonal variations, then, that the months of January and September have been chosen. January used to be a low point, whereas September was one of the good months, with a high level of employment.

The total number of articles printed in those two months is therefore taken as being representative for the year in question. Annual totals are not presented here, but in principle an approximation of the number of articles published in a given year can be found by multiplying the total for the two months by six.

The material used is housed in the collection at the Royal Danish Library Newspaper Reading Room, where copies of all issues of the two papers are kept on microfilm. The work of reading the microfilms on screen was carried out by a group of students of librarianship who were well versed in information search techniques. These students all received exactly the same instructions for data collection so as to ensure that their work processes were as uniform as possible.

The analysis also makes use of annual unemployment statistics, both in terms of the percentage of those with unemployment insurance who were unemployed in any given year, and the percentage of the total workforce. These statistical time series are presented here in an integrated graphical form drawn up by Mark Gervasini Nielsen MSc (Economics), a former research assistant at the Rockwool Foundation Research Unit. The data used for the time series are obtained from Statistics Denmark[9] and from Niels Kærgård.[10]

The reason for comparing the trends in the unemployment statistics and the intensity of the debate in the coverage by the two newspapers is to show whether there is a systematic correlation between the level of unemployment and the intensity of the debate in two newspapers with differing political standpoints. In addition, the curves give an overview of the level of interest in the two newspapers over 90 years of the twentieth century.

---

[9] Danmarks Statistik (1996).
[10] Kærgård (1991).

Results

Figure 1.1. is a graphical presentation of the number of items linked to unemployment recorded in *Berlingske Tidende* and *Social-Demokraten/Aktuelt*.

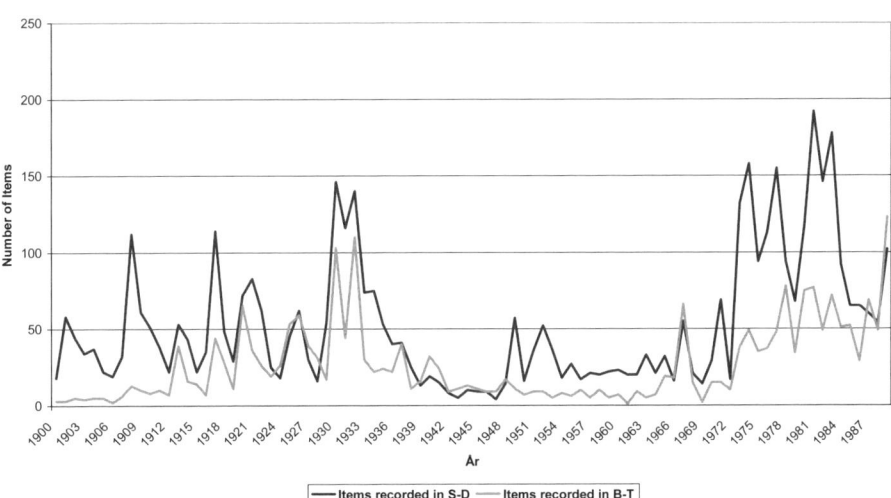

Source: The Rockwool Foundation Research Unit

One scarcely surprising conclusion is that the number of items in *Social-Demokraten/Aktuelt* either slightly or considerably exceeds the number in *Berlingske Tidende* in most of the years of the survey.

In the period up until the outbreak of the First World War, coverage of the topic of unemployment is found only to a limited degree in *Berlingske Tidende*, while the topic is covered extensively in *Social-Demokraten*. This, too, can hardly be considered surprising, since *Social-Demokraten* had begun all-out coverage of the subject in the mid-1870s, unemployment being a critical – if not *the* critical – social issue for many of the paper's readers.[11] For the trade union movement,

---

[11] In "Pressen og arbejdsløshedslovgivningen" (The press and unemployment legislation) (1946), Gustav Pedersen gives the following explanation of why not only *Berlingske Tidende*, but all the conservative papers toned down their coverage of the subject prior to 1914: "If a person should wish to undertake the disagreeable task of reading through all the Liberal and Conservative papers from the period between the turn of the century and the First World War, he or she will not find many articles that deal with the question of unemployment as something requiring state initiatives (....). During this period there was only a slight chance that benefits would bring about a situation

unemployment benefit was an important element in wage bargaining, since it ensured that unemployed workers would not be tempted to undercut the normal cost of labour in order to survive.

There are exceptions to the general tendency for *Social-Demokraten/Aktuelt* to devote more space to the issue than *Berlingske Tidende*. Such exceptions occurred in the years 1925 and 1926, during the first Social Democrat government, and in 1929, when in April the Social Democrats together with the Social Liberals again managed to take over the reins of government, though the differences are marginal. One possible explanation for the more intensive references to the unemployed is that unemployment may have become a politically opportune topic for the large right-of-centre newspapers to use in confrontation with the Social Democrat government – just as it had been good material for the Social Democrats in opposition, when major campaigns during periods of high unemployment had formed part of the *raison d'être* for the party and the unions.

A similar situation might have been expected to occur in the 1930s, but this was not the case. It may be that the crisis of the period was considered so threatening to the entire system that the editorial team of *Berlingske Tidende* chose to give the topic of unemployment less prominence than *Social-Demokraten*, though *Berlingske Tidende* by no means excluded unemployment from its columns. The Social Democrat paper, in contrast, was simply unable to give the topic less prominence, since it was so crucial for the party and the unions that the readers were kept informed of developments, and that the newspaper's editorial views would determine its readers' interpretations of events. Unemployment fell after 1933 and could thus be seen as having become a less pressing social problem, and one that overwhelmingly affected the unskilled; these factors were then reflected in the decreasing intensity of the debate in both the papers over the remainder of the decade – in particular in the case of *Berlingske Tidende*, but also clearly enough in *Social-Demokraten*.

The other period in which coverage was a fraction more intensive in *Berlingske Tidende* than in *Social-Demokraten* was during the German occupation. *Social-Demokraten* and the trade unions kept themselves tightly restrained in the public debate during the war years for fear of the occupying power. In other occupied countries, Social Democratic parties had been outlawed and union activities

---

where there were not enough workers for whom the risk of unemployment for even a short period was not such a great problem that they would allow themselves to be pressured into accepting low wages. It is therefore not only understandable, but in truth the logical consequence of the attitude of the employers, that the subject only became topical in the press at the same time as the unemployment funds enjoyed their extraordinarily rapid growth, and the rates of benefit increased, in the years 1918-19. It was then for the first time that large numbers of the lowest paid workers dared to say no to unreasonable conditions of employment" (p. 7).

severely restricted. The editors of *Social-Demokraten* had thus been rather reticent concerning the issue of unemployment, perhaps also in order to avoid drawing attention to the unemployed; the German occupying power might demand that labour be exported to Germany, where the labour market was desperate for more manpower. Similar considerations probably also applied for *Berlingske Tidende*, since the level of coverage in both newspapers was extremely low.[12]

Discussion in *Social-Demokraten/Aktuelt* was significantly greater in volume than in *Berlingske Tidende* during the years up until 1914, with the crisis year of 1909 as a high-point during this period; in the last years of the First World War; in the first three years of the 1920s; in the 50s; in most of the years of the 60s, and from the start of the oil crisis until the mid-1980s.

The unemployment figures

The graph curves in Figure 1.1. for the two papers' coverage of the theme of "the unemployed" from 1900 to 1990 show some very considerable fluctuations, and it is tempting to interpret these intuitively as an expression of changes in the level of unemployment. Such intuitive interpretation, however, is not necessarily reflected in the facts.

In 1987 the historian Alan Booth carried out an analysis for the United Kingdom similar to this one for Denmark.[13] One point that Booth makes is that in the intra-war years, the topic of "the unemployed" peaked in the British working class papers during the election campaign of 1929, when the level of unemployment was actually at its lowest level for the 1920s. The fact that the theme reached its peak in terms of newspaper coverage in 1929, and not during the tough times of the economic crisis of the 1930s, Booth explains by referring to the fact that the mass unemployment of the 1930s split the Labour Party politically. In other words, there need not necessarily be a direct correspondence between the level of unemployment and the priority given to the issue in the media.

In order to examine the relationship between the unemployment figures for Denmark and coverage in the newspapers, Figure 1.2. shows the levels of unemployment for the years between 1900 and 2000, given in percentages of people with unemployment insurance and of the entire labour force.

---

[12] The third period during which *Berlingske Tidende* devoted slightly more coverage to the topic of unemployment was from 1967 to 1968 and a fourth episode appeared in 1988.

[13] Booth (1987). Only a few such quantitative analyses have ever been carried out in relation to Denmark, and none of them on this topic. One example of a successful quantitative analysis of this kind can be found in the work of Jette D. Søllinge (1995).

Appendix 1

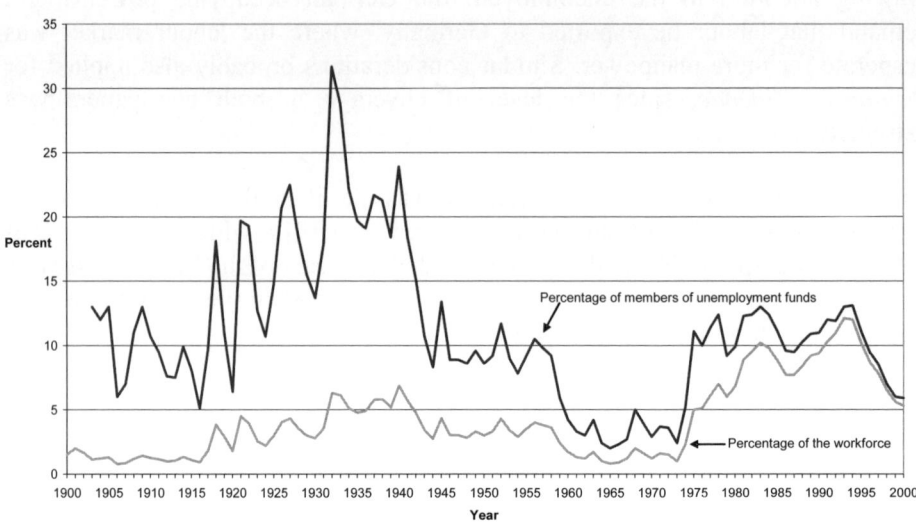

Figure 1.2. Percentages unemployed, 1900-2000

Source: Danmarks Statistik (1996), Kærgård (1991)

The statistics are a little uncertain for the early years of the period, and it should also be noted that the statistical basis for calculating the figures changed somewhat over time. In general, with respect to the unemployed percentage of those with unemployment insurance, the chart gives an impression of how:

- unemployment levels among the insured varied drastically up until the First World War

- a high point was reached in 1918

- the level rose suddenly in 1921 in the wake of the international peace crisis and then remained at a high but varying level throughout the 1920s

- unemployment reached new heights in 1932-33, when almost one insured worker in three was without a job

- the war years brought improved levels of employment, without however eliminating the problem of unemployment

- unemployment remained at a persistently high level throughout the 1950s, though it was below the levels of the 1920s and 1930s

- full employment first came to Denmark with the almost unbroken years of prosperity in the 1960s

- the oil crisis of 1973 was followed by persistently high levels of unemployment for the remainder of the period.

Unemployment only began to fall after 1995, heading towards the good levels of employment that we saw around 2008.

It is also evident from Figure 1.2. that the percentage of unemployed relative to the entire workforce was significantly lower than that relative to those with unemployment insurance until the oil crisis of 1973 and the introduction in 1979 of the early retirement scheme, which was dependent on membership of an unemployment fund, brought the number of the insured close to being identical to the total number of people in the workforce. Another factor bringing the two curves closer to one another was the decline in the number of the self-employed which resulted from the structural rationalisation of farming and the retail sector. From the beginning of the 1990s onwards, it makes little difference which method is used for calculating the level of unemployment.

The relationship between the unemployment figures and coverage in *Berlingske Tidende*

Figures 1.3. and 1.4. present overviews of the possible relationships between the numbers of newspaper items and the trends in unemployment statistics for *Berlingske Tidende* and *Social-Demokraten/Aktuelt*.

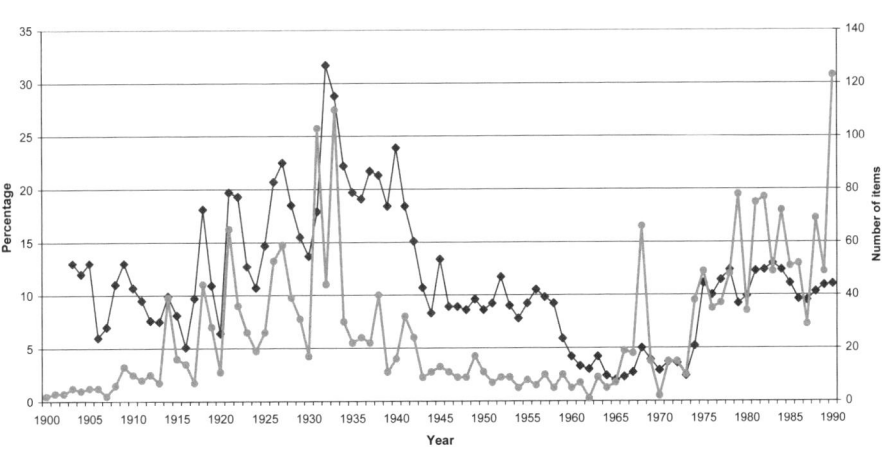

Figure 1.3. The relationship between fluctuations in the percentage unemployed and the number of items on the topic of "the unemployed" in Berlingske Tidende, 1900-1990

Source: The Rockwool Foundation Research Unit

In interpreting Figure 1.3., it is relevant to consider a number of different periods, as follows.

For the period up until 1914 there is no marked relationship between variations in the level of unemployment and the number of items on the topic in *Berlingske Tidende*. There are however rather more items in 1909 than in previous years, and this is probably the result of the attention aroused by the Syndicalist actions in the building trades and the resulting reaction in the political system, with initiatives for more laws and for public works projects.

In 1914 the outbreak of war and the general uncertainty about shortages of supplies contributed to the topic of the unemployed being covered in a relatively large number of items. This level of interest was greater than can be explained simply by changes in the numbers out of work. From 1914 to 1933, it is possible to trace a relatively close correlation between the unemployment figures and the number of items in *Berlingske Tidende*. From 1934, the topic of the unemployed was rather downplayed by the paper until the recession of 1968. The paper's coverage never quite returned to the same low levels as before 1914, but it was not far off, if we ignore a few isolated years in the 1930s and the 1940s.

The year 1968 was thus an exception to the generally low level of coverage up until 1974, when the rapidly rising unemployment figures caused a sharp increase in the number of items about the topic in *Berlingske Tidende*. A contributory explanation for the low priority given to the topic by the paper for long periods in which there was relatively high unemployment among those with unemployment insurance may well be that this group did not form part of the core readership of the paper. Until the 1960s unemployment measured as a percentage of the total workforce lay well below the equivalent figure for the insured.

A further contributory factor might be that *Berlingske Tidende* did not have the same need as *Social-Demokraten* to distance itself from revolutionary groups that sought to profit politically by mobilising the unemployed (see below).

In more general terms, it looks as though from the mid-1930s until 1968 and again from 1969 to 1973 *Berlingske Tidende* saw no reason to include unemployment among the most important social issues to which it devoted editorial space. As mentioned in previous sections, unemployment measured as a percentage of the entire workforce was much lower during this period than the figure for unemployment measured as a percentage of members of unemployment funds.

Nevertheless it is worth noting, as documented in previous sections, that for limited periods, for example during election campaigns, coverage of the unemployment issue could increase rapidly in significance in this moderate Conservative paper.

The relationship between the unemployment figures and coverage in *Social-Demokraten/Aktuelt*

The relationship between the economic cycle and coverage of the topic of unemployment in *Social-Demokraten/Aktuelt* is apparent from Figure 1.4.

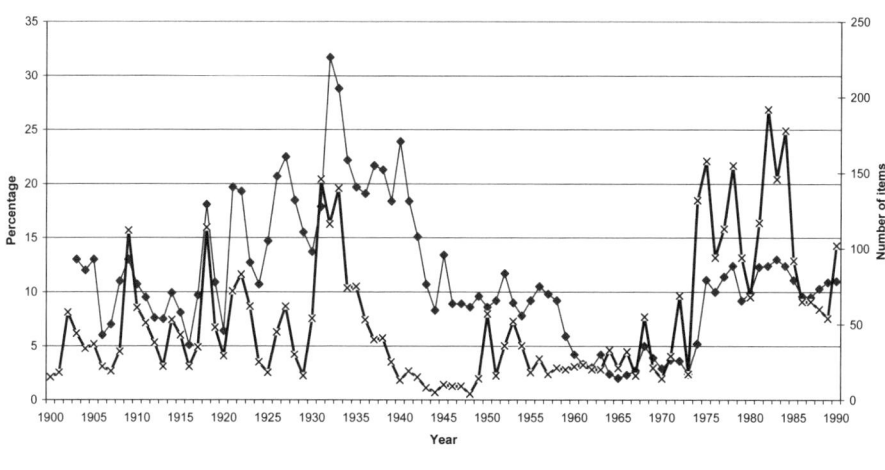

Figure 1.4. The relationship between fluctuations in the percentage unemployed and the number of items on the topic of "the unemployed" in Social-Demokraten/Aktuelt, 1900-1990

Source: The Rockwool Foundation Research Unit

From 1903, the first year for which figures are available for unemployment among members of unemployment funds, until 1935 there is a strong correlation between the unemployment rates among insured workers and the number of items about the unemployed in the paper. The number of items about the unemployed is greatest in relation to the unemployment figures for 1909 and 1918, when the Social Democratic movement had felt itself threatened by the tough arguments and actions of the Syndicalist far left. The number of items is relatively low for those years in the 1920s when the Social Democrats formed the government. However, overall the shapes of the two curves are amazingly close. The core readership of the paper was, as mentioned previously, organised labour, and it was vital for this target group to be fully informed regarding unemployment trends. Politically, it was very important for the paper to be able to show its readers that the Social Democratic Party and the unions were being active in making demands on the state and the local authorities that they should take action during periods of rising or high unemployment.

In the period after 1935 until 1950 there is a certain relationship between the two curves, but the number of items in the paper was relatively lower – even much lower – than in the period before 1935.

One of the main reasons for this situation in the last half of the 1930s was the paper's unwillingness to contribute to the destabilisation of one of Europe's few remaining democracies through too much discussion of the unemployed and of the social problems that were linked to the phenomenon of unemployment. According to both the Communists and the National Socialists, widespread unemployment was the strongest argument for the overthrow of democracy and the installation of a dictatorship – either "red" or "brown". To counter the rapidly expanding totalitarian movements, the Social Democrats and unions wanted to maintain "the inner defence" by emphasising the social responsibility and freedom to be enjoyed under a democracy led by Social Democrats and Social Liberals.

During the occupation, the fear that the Germans might export unemployed Danish labour to Germany on a major scale came into play, probably in combination with a general feeling within the Social Democratic and trade union movement that it was politic to keep a low profile with respect to social topics during an anti-Socialist occupation.

In the 1950s the number of items in the paper concerning unemployment was relatively high, and again largely followed changes in the level of unemployment. In the 1960s there were relatively few items published. For the year 1968 there is an increase in the number of items, almost certainly as a consequence of the rising unemployment figures, the fact that unemployment was the principal issue in the election campaign in January 1968, and the increasingly widespread fear that the good times were coming to an end.

After 1974 the number of items concerning the unemployed once again became heavily dependent on the economic cycle, and in general the theme was relatively well covered. It should be noted that this was the time when unemployment as a percentage of the entire labour force was approaching the percentage of those who were insured.

Summary and conclusions

It is apparent from the data that the correlation between fluctuations in the percentage of those with unemployment insurance who were out of work and the number of items published that were related to unemployment was much stronger in *Social-Demokraten/Aktuelt* than it was in *Berlingske Tidende* during the period 1900-1990. One explanation for this could be that organised labour formed the core readership of *Social-Demokraten/Aktuelt* and that these workers were also the most active supporters of the labour movement. The exceptions to this general pattern regarding the two papers were the periods in which special political considerations applied, namely the second half of the 1930s and the period of the occupation. At these times, the extremes in the political circumstances probably brought about a change in editorial priorities, reducing the number of items published concerning the unemployed.

Throughout the period considered here, the number of items published was considerably greater in *Social-Demokraten/Aktuelt* than in *Berlingske Tidende*. The few years in which the reverse was the case were those in which a Social Democrat government was in power, and the theme of "the unemployed" was a fairly permanent element in the opposition's critique of the Social Democrat government.

References

Booth, Alan. 1987. "Unemployment and Interwar Politics", in Sean Glynn and Alan Booth (eds). 1987. *The Road to Full Employment*. London: Allan & Unwin.

Danmarks Statistik. 1996. "Arbejdsløshedsserier 1910-1995". *Statistiske Efterretninger – Arbejdsmarked 1996:28*.

Jensen, Bent. 2006. *Træk af avisdebatten om de arbejdsløse fra 1840'erne til 1940'erne.* Volume I: *Debatten indtil 1907*. Copenhagen: The Rockwool Foundation Research Unit.

Jensen, Bent. 2007. *Træk af avisdebatten om de arbejdsløse fra 1840'erne til 1940'erne.* Volume II: *Debatten fra 1907 til 1940'erne*. Copenhagen: The Rockwool Foundation Research Unit.

Jensen, Bent. 2008. *Træk af avisdebatten om de arbejdsløse fra 1950'erne til 1990'erne*. Odense: University Press of Southern Denmark.

Kærgård, Niels. 1991. *Økonomisk vækst. En økonometrisk analyse af Danmark 1870-1981*. Copenhagen: Jurist- og Økonomforbundets Forlag.

Pedersen, Gustav. 1946. *Pressen og Arbejdsløshedslovgivningen*. Copenhagen: *Social-Demokraten*.

Søllinge, Jette D. 1995. *Dagspressens indholdsmæssige strukturudvikling 1983-1994 generelt såvel som med særligt henblik på lokaljournalistik og politikernes rolle i pressen*. Copenhagen: Statsministeriets medieudvalg.

Appendix 2

An overview of the newspapers in the survey

This appendix first describes the central, primarily national, papers used in the survey. The place of publication is stated for papers outside Copenhagen. This presentation is largely based on the work of Jette D. Søllinge and Niels Thomsen (1988, 1989 and 1991).

Berlingske Tidende was first published in 1749, originally as an evening paper and from 1847 with a morning edition as well, which later became the more important of the two. In 1913 the two publications separated definitively, with the evening edition continuing under an independent title until it ceased publication as a daily paper in 1971, though in part it has continued to appear in the form of *Weekendavisen*. At the outset, the paper was loyal to the state, and after 1848 it developed into a moderately conservative publication, seldom expressing itself in polemical style. It supported the Conservatives until 1949, after which time it declared itself to be an independent conservative paper. In terms of news coverage it was a leading publication from 1838, though perhaps with a degree of weakness from 1880 until 1913, when it was relaunched in the spirit of the press reform. From the early days, the paper was regarded as the newspaper of the business community, city dwellers, and civil servants. Today, its readers are primarily senior executives and businessmen.

Fyns Tidende (Odense; regional paper for Funen) was published between 1872 and 1979. The newspaper was linked to the Liberals (from 1890 to 1910 to the parliamentary group of Moderate Liberals). With its solid footing among country-dwellers, especially farm-owners, with its content based on solid political information and Grundtvigian principles, and with its hostile bias against the pseudo-radical "European" Liberals, *Fyns Tidende* enjoyed success through its consistent loyalty to the moderate wing of the Liberal Party. In 1902 and for a short while thereafter, *Fyns Tidende* was in terms of circulation the largest provincial daily paper, carrying much influence through its articles regarding the party line. The paper maintained its position as a political trend-setter up until around 1950, whereafter it became rather more set in its editorial ways.

Jyllands-Posten (Århus) was founded in 1871. At the outset it was a provincial paper covering Jutland, in particular the eastern parts; and from 1935, after the opening of the first bridge between Jutland and Funen, it also covered Funen. This local basis was manifested in the paper's support of specifically Jutlandic commercial interests. During the 1960s the newspaper underwent a drastic editorial modernisation, and eventually the paper became truly national in its coverage. Originally the newspaper was politically independent, but in 1877 it declared its support for the Right, later known as the Conservatives. Since 1938 it has been an independent middle-class paper. Throughout its existence, the paper has been known for its distinctive standpoints, and it has been a staunch supporter of economic liberalism. In terms of content, the paper has focused on politics and business news, in recent years supplemented with a certain amount of culture and debate. The readership profile tends towards the self-employed and senior executives.

Politiken first appeared in 1884 as a mouthpiece for the more radical circles among the Liberals – the "European" Liberals, led for the first 15 years of their existence by the editor of the paper, Viggo Hørup – before aligning itself with the newly-formed Social Liberals in 1905. In 1970 the paper declared itself to be independent social liberal, a line that it has maintained ever since. Especially after the closure of *Aktuelt* in 2001, the paper has positioned itself solidly on the left of the political spectrum. The paper's makeover in 1905 was the first fully developed example of the press reform. Political opinion-shaping was played down in favour of news, and the paper's interest in new and diverse topics was extended, especially with respect to social and human-interest issues. In particular, the paper gave priority to its own independent news coverage, in contrast to the previously prevailing situation whereby most papers simply copied material from each other. The reform also meant a wider spectrum of types of article, with news reports, background articles and interviews all becoming much more prominent. *Politiken* has always aimed to employ a large editorial staff, and their profile has helped it to maintain its image as a cultural paper, a paper for intellectuals. The core readership is socio-demographically diverse, but geographically primarily urban. Readers are to an increasing extent to be found among salaried employees.

Social-Demokraten/Aktuelt was launched as a daily paper in 1872 under the name *Socialisten*, but from May 1874 it adopted the name *Social-Demokraten* and was published with trade union support. In 1959 it changed its name to *Aktuelt* (from 1987 to 1997 *Det fri Aktuelt*). The paper ceased publication in April 2001. In the paper's declaration of intent the first editor, Louis Pio, stated that the journalists wished to write consistently from a workers' standpoint, and that the paper intended to base its news from the provinces on contributions from its own local correspondents, unlike the other Copenhagen papers, which mostly just lifted material from the provincial papers. Furthermore, Pio continued, there would be articles by well-known European socialists. The paper, like the party, was affiliated to the international socialist movement. Throughout its years of publication the paper was the mouthpiece of the Social Democrats, as evidenced by the large quantity of political material it printed and the less clear-cut distinction it made between news and comment than was normal in the national press. *Social-Demokraten*, which enjoyed great success in terms of circulation and to some extent financially during the period 1880-1914, was the country's largest paper during the first decade of the twentieth century. Thereafter, however, it found itself increasingly in need of financial support from the trade unions – in part, this was because the resources of the paper were used on establishing party papers throughout the country rather than on consolidating its own position. After the Second World War in particular the paper found it difficult to maintain its circulation, since it had not followed the rest of the press in depoliticisation and other forms of modernisation. A relaunch in 1987 came too late, and the paper never achieved editorial independence. The readers were primarily skilled and unskilled labourers, and from around 1950 increasingly also salaried staff and pensioners. Because of the nature of the topic discussed in this study paper, *Social-Demokraten/Aktuelt* is often the paper from which most material is taken.

Vestkysten was formed in 1918 through the merger of two small local papers, and it rapidly increased its circulation. In political terms it was a notable mouthpiece for the Liberals, becoming the party's most important press organ from around 1950 onward. In January 1991 it merged with the Conservative *Jydske Tidende* to form *JydskeVestkysten*, a politically-independent middle-class paper and the only paper covering the southern part of Jutland as far as Varde/Kolding.

The other newspapers which are drawn on as supplementary material in the analysis are the following:

Almuevennen was published once or twice per week during the years 1842-1856 (from January 1853 under the name *Folkebladet*). The paper had a circulation of less than 1,000, and was the press organ of the embryonic smallholders' movement. Its views were Liberal-Democratic, and the smallholders' movement formed a leading element in its content.

Dagens Nyheder was published from 1868 onwards as a Conservative Party paper, and up until 1873 in part as a popular daily. In 1889 it was bought up by C. Ferslew as a supplement to *Nationaltidende*.

Flyve Posten was published over the years 1845-1870 as a Conservative daily paper, up until 1852 also with traces of the popular press about it. After that date it became a national paper of Conservative opinion. Circulation increased from an original 7,000 to around 10,000 in 1852, after which it declined steadily.

Fædrelandet (National Liberal) appeared as a weekly paper from 1834, and as a daily from 1839. From the outset, the paper was a notable organ of the National Liberals, and its columns were totally dominated by comment, with special weight on the communication of political principles, while news was ignored. It saw itself as "the recognised authoritative mouthpiece for and the concrete link to the National Liberal Party",[14] and it placed strong emphasis on the nationality

---

[14] Stender-Petersen (1978, p. 14).

campaign in Schleswig, on the Scandinavian movement, on farm reform and on the demand for a free constitution. The paper was thus an organ for the political opposition to Absolutism; in consequence, several issues were impounded and it was fined on various occasions up until 1848. The academic style of writing used by the paper, with long, demanding articles, made the paper an elite publication with a small circulation, but great prestige, until 1864. In the years that followed it neither could nor would reform itself, and it closed in 1882.

Fædrelandet (National Socialist) appeared from January 1939 until 4 May 1945 as the national paper of the Danish National Socialist Party. The paper was the official mouthpiece of the party, and the content was primarily political propaganda. Such news material as it published was also strongly politically tinted, and the editorial comment was marked in part by uncritical admiration for everything connected with the National Socialists and the Third Reich and in part by provocative abuse of any political opposition, which often crossed over into informer activity. Despite massive German subsidies, the paper ran at a loss. The print run paralleled German fortunes in the war. Circulation rose from an original 4,000 to over 12,000 in September 1940 and 23,000 by the end of 1940, before falling to 14,000 in 1943 and 10,000 in 1944.

Kjøbenhavnsposten was founded in 1827 as a cultural publication, but became in the 1830s the representative for the Liberal opposition to the left of the National Liberals, whose press organ *Fædrelandet* the paper criticised for being too nationalistic and for betraying the democratic movement. The paper, which never had more than around 500 subscribers, introduced socialist writers and politicians to Danish readers and raised various social issues, including the smallholders' demands for land reform in the 1840s and the social and political concerns of the workers. In the run-up to 1848 the paper developed into a representative of the radical-democratic forces, and it championed the cause of the rights of the capital over country districts on the basis of the assumption that Copenhagen would pave the way for a social revolution in the wake of the introduction of democracy. After 1849 there was a massive shift in the opinions of the paper, which from then on became national conservative and royalist; the editor, J.P.M. Grüne, saw the power of the monarchy as a bulwark against the advance of capitalism, which was regarded as a threat to craftsmen in particular. The paper ceased publication in 1856, and an attempt to relaunch it in 1858 lasted for less than a year.

Nationaltidende was launced in 1876. In 1931 it was merged with *Dagens Nyheder* and continued publication under that title. The paper continued to appear until 1961 (from 1936 to 1954 once again under the name *Nationaltidende*). It was conservative in its stance, and was popular with the middle classes, especially until around 1931. From 1936 onward it was owned by and associated with members of the business community, in particular the Industrial Council and the Danish Confederation of Employers.

Solidaritet was published as a weekly paper from 16 December 1911 and as a daily from November 1918 until May 1921. It was the press organ of the Syndicalist worker opposition to Social Democrats and everything to the right of it, and to parliamentary democracy in general. The paper enjoyed a brief period of success, with circulation rising to a peak of 17,000 in 1919. In May 1921 it was merged with the Communist daily paper *Arbejdet* (published 1920-21) to form *Arbejderbladet*, which was published from 1921 to 1922, then as a weekly from 1922 to 1934, and then daily again from 1934 to 1941 as the press organ of the Danish Communist Party. In 1941 it was banned on German orders, but publication restarted in 1945 and continued until 1990 under the name *Land og Folk*. An illegal edition of *Land og Folk* began publication under the title *Politiske Maanedsbreve* in July 1941; it was distributed in manuscript form to a number of groups all over the country who recopied or printed it. The circulation varied from between 250 and 600 in the beginning of the period, increasing to 4,000 in April 1945. The number of readers, however, was significantly greater, as copies were passed from hand to hand. An estimate of the readership would be 5 to 10 households for each copy. These papers were primarily organs of propaganda, and the relatively modest news content was constantly subordinated to campaigning material.

The newspapers covered by this survey made up a major part of the total Danish daily press output. On the basis of the circulation of the selected papers alone, as shown in the table on page 62, there can be no question that the analysis must have succeeded in capturing the main trends in the debate on the unemployed, just as the debate in these papers did not simply reflect the fact that the topic was on the political agenda, but actively contributed to it being there. In addition, the newspapers selected are representative of the dominant political and commercial forces of the day throughout the period, including the trade union movement and important groupings among the employers.

Table 1.1. Circulation figures for the newspapers in the survey (daily, in thousands)

	Berlingske Tidende [1]	Politiken	Social-Demokraten/ Aktuelt [2]	Jyllands-Posten	Fyns Tidende	(Jydske) Vestkysten	Dagens Nyheder [3]	Arbejderbladet [4]/ Land & Folk	Fædrelandet	Morgenbladet
1830	approx. 2	-	-	-	-	-	-	-	-	-
1845	3.6	-	-	-	-	-	-	-	approx. 1.5	-
1858	approx. 8	-	-	-	-	-	-	-	approx. 1.7	-
1870	8.8	-	-	-	-	-	-	-	approx. 1.5	-
1880	13.0	-	3.0	approx. 2	1.7	-	approx. 3.5	-	max. 1.5	approx. 2
1890	13.0	12.1	22.0	approx. 2-3	3.7	-	14.0	-	-	2-3
1901	16.2	23.1	42.0	3.5	8.4	-	10.0	-	-	-
1913	16.4	50.4	46.1	7.0	12.5	-	13.2	-	-	-
1920	44.0	63.0	62.0	20.7	16.4	8.6	approx. 40	2.6	-	-
1930	93.0	80.0	67.0	22.6	24.4	15.8	approx. 40	-	-	-
1943	162.0	134.0	55.0	40.5	29.7	29.5	47.4	-	-	-
1953	163.0	148.0	43.0	68.9	32.5	34.4	33.6	17.6	-	-
1963	171.0	137.0	41.0	61.9	35.5	44.1	-	7.0	-	-
1973	146.0	121.0	53.0	79.2	23.4	54.0	-	8.5	-	-
1983	118.0	149.8	54.6	102.2	-	55.8	-	10.0	-	-
1993	134.4	152.1	41.3	145.6	-	96.2	-	-	-	-
2000	154.8	140.5	25.9	179.5	-	90.3	-	-	-	-

Sources: Søllinge and Thomsen (1988, 1989, 1991), Dansk Oplagsbulletin and Dansk Oplagskontrol.
[1] Morning edition.
[2] Including provincial editions 1920-30.
[3] *Dagens Nyheder/Nationaltidende* – see above.
[4] In 1920, the paper's forerunner *Arbejdet* (merged with *Solidaritet* to form *Arbejderbladet*).

References

Stender-Petersen, Ole. 1978. *"Kjøbenhavnsposten" – organ for "det extreme Democrati"*. Odense: Odense Universitetsforlag.

Søllinge, Jette D. 2003. "Et gjaldende Signal til Folkerejsning". *Rotunden*, No. 18, 2003.

Søllinge, Jette D. and Niels Thomsen. 1988, 1989 og 1991. *De danske aviser 1634-1989/91, volumes 1-3*. Odense: Odense Universitetsforlag.

Publications in English from the Rockwool Foundation Research Unit

Time and Consumption
Edited by Gunnar Viby Mogensen. With contributions by Søren Brodersen, Thomas Gelting, Niels Buus Kristensen, Eszter Körmendi, Lisbeth Pedersen, Benedicte Madsen. Niels Ploug, Erik Ib Schmidt, Rewal Schmidt Sørensen, and Gunnar Viby Mogensen (Statistics Denmark, Copenhagen. 1990)

Danes and Their Politicians
By Gunnar Viby Mogensen (Aarhus University Press. 1993)

Solidarity or Egoism?
By Douglas A. Hibbs (Aarhus University Press. 1993)

Welfare and Work Incentives. A North European Perspective
Edited by A.B. Atkinson and Gunnar Viby Mogensen. With Contributions by A.B. Atkinson, Richard Blundell, Björn Gustafsson, Anders Klevmarken, Peder J. Pedersen, and Klaus Zimmermann (Oxford University Press. 1993)

Unemployment and Flexibility on the Danish Labour Market
By Gunnar Viby Mogensen (Statistics Denmark, Copenhagen. 1994)

On the Measurement of a Welfare Indicator for Denmark 1970-1990
By Peter Rørmose Jensen and Elisabeth Møllgaard (Statistics Denmark, Copenhagen. 1995)

The Shadow Economy in Denmark 1994. Measurement and Results
By Gunnar Viby Mogensen, Hans Kurt Kvist, Eszter Körmendi, and Søren Pedersen (Statistics Denmark, Copenhagen. 1995)

Work Incentives in the Danish Welfare State: New Empirical Evidence
Edited by Gunnar Viby Mogensen. With contributions by Søren Brodersen, Lisbeth Pedersen, Peder J. Pedersen, Søren Pedersen, and Nina Smith (Aarhus University Press. 1995)

Actual and Potential Recipients of Welfare Benefits with a Focus on Housing Benefits, 1987-1992
By Hans Hansen and Marie Louise Hultin (Statistics Denmark, Copenhagen. 1997)

The Shadow Economy in Western Europe. Measurement and Results for Selected Countries
By Søren Pedersen. With contributions by Esben Dalgaard and Gunnar Viby Mogensen (Statistics Denmark, Copenhagen. 1998)

Immigration to Denmark. International and National Perspectives
By David Coleman and Eskil Wadensjö. With contributions by Bent Jensen and Søren Pedersen (Aarhus University Press. 1999)

Nature as a Political Issue in the Classical Industrial Society: The Environmental Debate in the Danish Press from the 1870s to the 1970s
By Bent Jensen (Statistics Denmark, Copenhagen. 2000)

Foreigners in the Danish newspaper debate from the 1870s to the 1990s
By Bent Jensen (Statistics Denmark, Copenhagen. 2001)

The integration of non-Western immigrants in a Scandinavian labour market: The Danish experience
By Marie Louise Schultz-Nielsen. With contributions by Olaf Ingerslev, Claus Larsen, Gunnar Viby Mogensen, Niels-Kenneth Nielsen, Søren Pedersen, and Eskil Wadensjö (Statistics Denmark, Copenhagen. 2001)

Immigration and the public sector in Denmark
By Eskil Wadensjö and Helena Orrje (Aarhus University Press. 2002)

Social security in Denmark and Germany – with a focus on access conditions for refugees and immigrants. A comparative study
By Hans Hansen, Helle Cwarzko Jensen, Claus Larsen, and Niels-Kenneth Nielsen (Statistics Denmark, Copenhagen. 2002)

The Shadow Economy in Germany, Great Britain, and Scandinavia. A measurement based on questionnaire surveys
By Søren Pedersen (Statistics Denmark, Copenhagen. 2003)

Do-it-yourself work in North-Western Europe. Maintenance and improvement of homes
By Søren Brodersen (Statistics Denmark, Copenhagen. 2003)

Migrants, Work, and the Welfare State
Edited by Torben Tranæs and Klaus F. Zimmermann. With contributions by Thomas Bauer, Amelie Constant, Horst Entorf, Christer Gerdes, Claus Larsen, Poul Chr. Matthiessen, Niels-Kenneth Nielsen, Marie Louise Schultz-Nielsen, and Eskil Wadensjö (University Press of Southern Denmark. 2004)

Black Activities in Germany in 2001 and in 2004. A Comparison Based on Survey Data
By Lars P. Feld and Claus Larsen (Statistics Denmark, Copenhagen. 2005)

From Asylum Seeker to Refugee to Family Reunification. Welfare Payments in These Situations in Various Western Countries
By Hans Hansen (Statistics Denmark, Copenhagen. 2006)

A Comparison of Welfare Payments to Asylum Seekers, Refugees, and Reunified Families. In Selected European Countries and in Canada
By Torben Tranæs, Bent Jensen, and Mark Gervasini Nielsen (Statistics Denmark, Copenhagen. 2006)

Employment Effects of Reducing Welfare to Refugees
By Duy T. Huynh, Marie Louise Schultz-Nielsen, and Torben Tranæs (The Rockwool Foundation Research Unit. 2007)

Determination of Net Transfers for Immigrants in Germany
By Christer Gerdes (The Rockwool Foundation Research Unit. 2007)

What happens to the Employment of Native Co-Workers when Immigrants are Hired?
By Nikolaj Malchow-Møller, Jakob Roland Munch, and Jan Rose Skaksen
(The Rockwool Foundation Research Unit. 2007)

Immigrants at the Workplace and the Wages of Native Workers
By Nikolaj Malchow-Møller, Jakob Roland Munch, and Jan Rose Skaksen
(The Rockwool Foundation Research Unit. 2007)

Crime and Partnerships
By Michael Svarer (University Press of Southern Denmark, The Rockwool Foundation Research Unit. 2008)

Immigrant and Native Children's Cognitive Outcomes and the Effect of Ethnic Concentration in Danish Schools
By Peter Jensen and Astrid Würtz Rasmussen (University Press of Southern Denmark, The Rockwool Foundation Research Unit. 2008)

The Unemployed in the Danish Newspaper Debate from the 1840s to the 1990s
By Bent Jensen (University Press of Southern Denmark, The Rockwool Foundation Research Unit. 2008)

The Rockwool Foundation Research Unit on the Internet

Completely updated information, e.g. about the latest projects of the Research Unit, can be found on the Internet on the home page of the Research Unit at the address:

www.rff.dk

The home page includes in a Danish and an English version:

- a commented survey of publications stating distributors of the books of the Research Unit

- survey of research projects

- information about the organization and staff of the Research Unit

- information about data base and choice of method and

- newsletters from the Research Unit

Printed newsletters from the Rockwool Foundation Research Unit can also be ordered free of charge on telephone +45 39 17 38 32.